To Mike,

Thank you for opening
your heart and mind to
all I am at the House of Mercy.

Sister Grace

A Place of Mercy:
Finding God on the Street

By: Thomas O'Brien

faithAlivebooks.com
spiritual and religious books

Grand Rapids, Michigan 49546

A Place of Mercy
Finding God on the Street
by Thomas O'Brien, Ph.D.

Editing by Sara Bosin Fink
Cover and book design by Leslie Littler

Copyright © 2004 by Thomas O'Brien, Ph.D.

Published by

faithAlivebooks
491 Prestwick Dr. SE
Grand Rapids, MI 49546
616.956.5044
www.faithAlivebooks.com
Daniel J. Pierson, founder

ISBN 0-9764221-0-7
Printed in the United States

For I was hungry and you gave me something to eat,
I was thirsty and you gave me something to drink,
I was a stranger and you invited me in,
I needed clothes and you clothed me,
I was sick and you looked after me,
I was in prison and you came to visit me ...

Matthew 25: 35—36

Contents:

Carpe Diem

It was a very cold January night when I arrived at the House of Mercy for the first time. I drove up to a small ramshackle house at the head of a T intersection and parked my car haphazardly among a few others in a muddy lot next door. I made my way through the clutter, the mud, and the snow banks to a makeshift front door that was in need of a knob. A light bulb over the front door revealed rotting pine clapboards, many just hanging like dead skin from the side of a wall that was leaning precariously inward and bowing away at the foundation. I knocked on the door only to find it had no latch and the modest force of my hand knocking was jarring the door open with each stroke. The door opened into a room teeming with people, all of whom were either too busy or too accustomed to strangers to pay attention to an intruder like me.

The musky odor of a mob held captive in a room designed for fewer occupants hung in every cubic inch of every room in that house. It consisted of sweat, urine, dirty diapers, dogs, cats, pot, crack, mildew, grease, fried chicken, saliva and a small plastic air freshener adorned with cheerful sunflower colors, whose presence was more ironic than effective. I wanted to ask someone where I might find Sr. Grace, but everyone seemed busy, or at least preoccupied.

Sr. Grace was a student at St. Bernard's Institute who had taken a couple of courses I taught and liked my perspectives on liberation theologies so much that she thought I might find a visit to her outreach to the poor and homeless interesting. She was a fiery, blond haired woman with boundless energy and a wild look in her eyes. She spoke uncompromisingly about the preferential option for the poor and she backed up those words with a long history of radical activism on the streets of Rochester, NY. That history reached back to the 1960's when she was a newly professed Sister of Mercy doing parish ministry in the northern slums of Rochester. From the start, Sr. Grace had an instinct for publicly recognizing the dignity of the poor and marginalized. The courageous character of her often-combative witness won for her a few dedicated followers, as well as many enemies in high places.

I spent the next few minutes milling around the impossibly cluttered front room attempting to make sense of this makeshift bizarre. No one seemed to know exactly where Sr. Grace was, but eventually a pointed-finger consensus began to take shape that she was located somewhere in the building, and more precisely, up a small three-step flight of stairs. In the room at the top of the stairs the Wheel of Fortune spun lucklessly on a TV surrounded by a huddled mass of the poor, yearning to be free.

Out of another room stepped a tall, dark, middle-aged, African American man with a purposeful stride. It occurred to me immediately that I was in his sights. Relief and apprehension mixed as I reached out my hand to greet my deliverer. He introduced himself as C.W.—a name I would struggle to discern for the next month or so. He led me into the room he had emerged from moments ago and there sat Sr. Grace behind a gray metal desk surrounded by an bevy of needy clients and busy disciples. Between giving attentive feedback to a woman whose utilities had been turned off, and explaining basic concepts of liberation theology to a couple of long term guests, Grace rose to greet me with her characteristic smile and hug. Upon greeting me she gave me the task of facilitating the discussion on themes of liberation so she could focus her energies on care-giving tasks. Being sensibly cautious, the remaining liberation discussion group and I instantly fell into a Mexican-standoff silence. Grace had mistakenly assumed that a healthy period of discussing weather reports and sports scores could be waived in these circumstances.

Silently I drank in my surroundings that included abused filing cabinets, neglected wood trim, and battered furnishings, all coated by one or more layers of sedimented funk. Amidst this featureless gray backdrop, Sr. Grace flickered and buzzed like a neon sign. As she sat poised on the edge of her chair behind the desk, she appeared ready to pounce on the next opportunity to advocate for the downtrodden.

My attention wandered to the other characters on this claustrophobic stage. The woman speaking to Sr. Grace spoke softly, yet clearly and articulately. Her demeanor was purposeful and earnest. She was adorned head to toe in thrift shop chic and her grooming was precise. She looked more like someone interviewing for a job, than a desperate mother of three seeking emergency assistance. I marveled at her courage and determination as it became clearer that she must have swallowed a large volume of pride to come and petition the House of Mercy for assistance.

The three men in the liberation theology support group had given up thinking of ways to break the ice with me and resumed a conversation among themselves in hushed voices. They were seated facing me in a row of chairs lined up against the wall. The man on my left was a middle-aged African American who clearly dressed to impress in spite of his generic beer budget. He had a low-cut sweater showing off numerous gold trinkets hanging around his scrawny neck. He was missing the lion's share of his teeth and he spoke a street dialect with a percussive, staccato rhythm that was, at the same time, slurred by the absence of teeth. It would be many months before Prince and I could carry on a conversation without an interpreter close at hand.

An older African American gentleman, who was also dark like Prince, sat directly in front of me leaning to one side in his armchair supporting his chin with his hand, giving his occasional nod a thoughtful aura in a conversation that was otherwise indecipherable to me. When he finally did speak, his words were nearly as slurred as Prince's because his mouth housed not a single tooth. His big graceful hands with long bony fingers would periodically envelope and caress his face in a slow and deliberate downward motion. Tricky Dick was an intelligent man, frustrated by a life punctuated by poverty, racism, addiction and inadequate opportunity.

To my right sat an African American man in his mid-thirties. He had a lighter complexion than Prince or Tricky Dick and he spoke in a deep baritone that resonated throughout the room, even when he was whispering. His pronunciation was as clear as the others' was sloppy. Greg was in constant motion, his hands and feet busy with one perseveration or another. He seemed excited and apparently impatient with the pace of the conversation. His head was always slightly bowed as if humbled by an unseen royal presence. His piercing and darting eyes betrayed the battle being waged within. Greg's needs were as simple to identify as they were difficult to meet. A healthy dose of confidence would have unlocked his substantial store of talent and goodwill. Until such a miracle could be procured, Greg would remain his own worst enemy.

"You have to say something before we leave," said Grace, her voice rising well above the din, as the assemble troops snapped to attention. Her eyes were fixed on me indicating I was the one to say "something." The look I flashed back must have sent the message of surprise, which I had not yet formulated into intelligible speech.

Seeing my dismay Grace elaborated, "Just tell us something about liberation from racism and poverty…Oh, and something about Martin Luther King." It was Martin Luther King Day after all. As she was completing her outline for my speech a round African American man in his mid-fifties with Pillsbury-Doughboy features called Sister Grace's name repeatedly from the doorway until he was acknowledged.

"The bus is ready," he said, "and everybody's waitin' on you."

Sister Grace blushed and flashed a shy smile as she assembled the things she would need to go out on this cold mid-winter night.

"Alright…thank you Tim." She said.

Looking at me she confided, "They're always waiting for me."

"Here Gracie," C.W. said as he swooped in through the doorway handing Sr. Grace her coat. He laid his free hand reassuringly on my shoulder and quipped,

"I hear you're going to be our speaker tonight."

"Uh…yeah." Said the orator. News appeared to travel at the speed of light in the House of Mercy. C.W.'s tone and delivery conveyed the message that I was not the first "volunteer" Sr. Grace had conscripted for impromptu duties.

In unison the occupants of Sr. Grace's office rose and joined the purposeful, yet chaotic beehive of activity, which would result in our reassembly back in the room where I had first entered. As we stepped down into the front room an exhausted, ragtag platoon greeted our advent in a marginalized mélange. The very presence of C.W. and the Sisters commanded discipline and soon the congregation was silent and attentive.

Sister Grace raised her hand and began a motivational address. She thanked everyone for coming out in the dark and the chill to participate in this event. From her brief description I concluded we were all going to a TV studio downtown where leaders in Rochester's African American community were to appear in an open forum to talk about the contributions of Martin Luther King. The picture that began to take shape in my mind was of a Catholic grade school field trip, complete with nuns, community leaders and that big yellow school bus idling at the front curb waiting to whisk us away for the evening's activity.

Grace's proud introduction of her theology professor jarred me out of my school days reverie. What poured forth from me that evening in that room has been mercifully repressed by a mortified psyche. Nevertheless, I do believe it followed the general outline laid out for me earlier by Grace. Remarkable only for its irrelevance, my prophecy concluded so inconclusively that the entire room sat silent for a bloated moment wondering whether or not I was finished. Finally, Sister Rita chimed into the awkward silence to lead us all in the Lord's Prayer. Thank God for rote prayer!

The brisk night air was bracing, yet nonetheless refreshing. The cold-sterilized mid-January air erased the humid warmth and rancid odor of this cooped up flock of humanity. The bare light bulb illumination in the House of Mercy had turned us all into bumbling zombies as we ventured into the darkness outside. We shuffled, stumbled and lurched our way toward the one visible light source of the bus headlights. It was a sight that would have made a B horror movie director salivate. We all gave a brief encore of our zombified characters when we stepped onto the bus and fumbled in complete darkness for a seat.

I sat next to a round woman in her late fifties, who seemed right at the same comfort level as I when it came to socializing in close quarters with complete strangers. She held her purse bunched up in her lap, and sat pressed against the window looking straight ahead as though she was awaiting further instructions. I tried to mimic her deportment—after all, she seemed to be a veteran of these events. We spent the rest of the bus trip looking away from one another, fighting the urge to make contact. Mrs. Washington and I would become friends one day soon, but tonight neither of us needed one more experience outside our respective comfort zones.

When the leadership team consisting of the three nuns, C.W. and a host of volunteers had taken their seats at the front, the bus pulled away, rocking, rumbling and jerking over the ragged pot-holed streets of the northern slums. Intermittently, Sister Grace would break the monotonous bus ride by standing and facing her captive followers proclaiming announcements, updates, corrections, or cheers of encouragement. Once or twice C.W. also made an announcement in his easy-going, matter-of-fact style, which contrasted so perfectly with Grace's strident and dramatic proclamations. In so many ways, C.W. was Sister Grace's straight man. Grace could make directions to the washroom sound compelling, while C.W., with his laid-back delivery, could turn the momentous into the mundane. Each style had its place at the House of Mercy where motivation to pursue small goals, and endurance to overcome significant obstacles were often in short supply.

We all knew we were nearing our destination as the bus left the rough roads of the slums behind and began to cruise the quiet, smooth pavement downtown. There were streetlights downtown that shed enough light for us to see one another, as well as the interior of the bus, for the first time that evening. I studied my environment for a moment trying to identify those things I had stumbled over, and those individuals I had inadvertently bumped into on the way to my seat. I also studied faces, postures and speech patterns attempting to discern the *esprit de corps* among the rank and file. I sensed an unusual mixture of anxiety and determination. I still had no idea what this trip was really all about so anxiety and determination just seemed out of place for a field trip, that, in my mind, was destined merely to passively witness community leaders speaking on TV about Martin Luther King.

My behavioral observations and research was cut short as the bus came to a halt in front of the entrance to the TV studio. The world we had left fifteen minutes ago would have virtually nothing in common with the world we were now entering. The pathetic bare light bulb illumination had been replaced by numerous fluorescent and high pressure sodium fixtures, successfully fighting back against the encroachment of night. The dangerous junk-strewn, snow-covered, mud lawn had been replaced by the efficient, swept and plowed, concrete sidewalk. The small, funky, familiar wood walls, doors, floors, and steps had been replaced by a world dominated by enormous sterilized, impersonal, glass, steel and concrete structures. Though I had seen these buildings before (or ones like them), this was the first time I had experienced them as intimidating. Through the broad glass doors I could see that the loose, free-flowing order of the House of Mercy beehive had been replaced by a more neurotic regimen in which a cadre of ushers ensured rigorous adherence to the minute details of time and space. I hesitated before exiting the bus, fighting back a fleeting sense of anxiety informing me that, for some unknown reason, I did not belong here.

I was met by C.W. at the bottom of the bus steps.

"I see you survived." He said with a warm smile and an easy shake of the hand.

"I did indeed." I said, trying to sound perky and unruffled.

"Grace, Rita and Gloria [the nuns] are already off doing their thing.

Unless you have other plans, I thought you might want to sit with me." He offered this invitation as he pulled me by the right hand he was shaking to take me out of the path of oncoming field trip participants exiting the bus. As I looked at his kind relaxed face, listened to his low resonant voice and fell into the rhythm of his delivery, my anxiety level immediately dropped and good humor returned. I accepted his gracious offer and spent the rest of the evening in the presence of a man blessed in a special way with the gift to calm and emotionally heal anyone, anywhere under almost any kind of circumstance.

Assuming I understood fully the purpose of this trip to the studio, C.W. said,

"Grace is giving the group a last minute pep talk and Rita and Gloria are trying to calm those who have cold feet."

I wondered why everyone would need a pep talk and what role our people might be playing which would produce so much anxiety. Clearly, something far more interesting than a field trip was afoot. Knowing Grace and her penchant for ruffling feathers I began to suspect the evening's activities would involve a lot more than the passive spectating that I was anticipating only moments before. Suddenly I really was feeling perky and unruffled. I was full of questions, but I didn't want to appear entirely out of the loop. How could I phrase my questions in such a way as to get basic information without appearing dumb?

"So what are the details of tonight's plan?" I asked, trying to cloak my general ignorance by focusing on my forgivable ignorance of the details.

"Didn't Gracie tell you what this was about?" C.W. asked, sidestepping my subtle deception entirely. As I searched for an even subtler recovery, C.W. forged ahead into a thorough summary of the real reason we had all ventured out into this forbidding, cold night. He outlined the evening's activities as we meandered into the front lobby of the studio where we were met by a serious and furtive Grace, who addressed us in a hushed voice.

"They have a microphone at the head of one of the isles and I was told they are still planning to take questions from the audience if there is time at the end of the prepared statements."

"Perfect, is Mary Jane OK?" Asked C.W. matter-of-factly.

With a reanimated voice and a jovial smile Grace said, "She'll be fiiiiiinnnnne." As Grace turned toward me, I found myself locked into her playful, mischievous gaze.

"Isn't this great!" She exclaimed. "Just like you said in class, the margins are about to erupt at the center! Right here at Channel 9 in

Rochester."

Grace, I would discover, was a very talented eruptor.

Now, with my own recently reanimated sense of anxiety, we moved from the lobby into the audience area of the studio and found a seat near the back. The rest of the group was already seated nearer the front and Grace soon left C.W. and me to resume her cheerleading role among the House of Mercy guests.

From the black ceiling hung stage lights of various shapes, sizes and colors. In back of us loomed cameras mounted on rolling pedestals and electronic production equipment neatly stacked in tall rack-mounted cases. Patch cords stuck out, crisscrossed, and hung suspended in a tangled web that made the otherwise expensive and professional equipment look like garbage piled up at a junkyard. We were seated in auditorium style seats bolted to a concrete floor that modestly angled downward toward the front stage. The stage itself was elevated about four feet and some of the guest speakers for this event had already taken their seats in the spotlights.

Other smaller groups of people were filing into the audience. The studio wasn't very large, possibly accommodating 200 people. Nonetheless, for this event there would be more than enough seats to go around. Two more speakers, a man and a woman, took the stage as the production crew and make-up staff quickly converged to prep the new arrivals. I looked at my watch and it was 6:54pm—the event would be starting in only six minutes. There was a buzz in the audience that eventually made its way to those of us in the back that Mayor Bill Johnson was the fifth and final speaker. The Mayor was notorious for arriving late at virtually every engagement he attended, and, true to form, the program was on the verge of starting without him and no one knew where he was. Stagehands and event hosts frantically consulted each other with alarmed expressions and exclamatory gestures.

Meanwhile, the other guest speakers calmly chatted with each other and read prepared statements to themselves, organizing their thoughts and memorizing catch phrases. All of the guest speakers were African Americans and performed various leadership roles in the community. To my shame, I didn't know any of them, but C.W. was able to fill in the gaps in my civic awareness. He also freely editorialized while identifying the speakers, giving me his personal impressions of the individuals, as well as his interpretation of their relationship to the House of Mercy. Sitting to the far left was a minister of one of the largest black Baptist churches in the city—probably the largest according to C.W. He was a tall thin man with chiseled features whose dapper appearance and self-possessed air matched C.W.'s characterization of him as pompous. He and the House of Mercy treated one another as irrelevant. Next to the minister sat an older overweight man, who had a darker complexion than the other panelists. Willie Lightfoot was a State Legislator who maintained a residence in a poor neighborhood in Rochester not far from the House of Mercy. C.W.'s portrayal of Mr. Lightfoot was significantly more flattering than that of the minister. With a few exceptions, Mr. Lightfoot had been an advocate for the poor and for the House of Mercy. Next to Mr. Lightfoot sat a beautiful, young, trim woman who was the evening news reporter for one of the rival TV stations in Rochester. C.W. knew very little about her other than the fact that she had done an informative mini-series a few years back on the Lewis Street Center—a community organization just down the street from the House of Mercy. An empty chair stood between the reporter and a young man in a brown suit sitting on the far right. Taylor Price, a Lewis Street Center caseworker possessed a rather light complexion and a very 'worked-out' physique, one that, according to C.W., matched more appropriately his career aspirations than his concern for the poor.

Just then my civics lesson was interrupted by the arrival of the star of the panel. With only two minutes to spare the Mayor trotted into the room flanked by a small entourage. A rather tall man with a commanding presence, he quickly apologized, was briefed about the plan for the evening's program, and took the empty seat on the stage just in time for the program to begin.

As a stagehand counted down to the start of the program, the house lights dimmed and the five panelists were joined by a discussion moderator—the news anchor for Channel 9—who was a light skinned man of mixed ancestry, small in stature and handsome in an exotic, bookish manner. He had a real stage presence and a calm, confident professionalism which gave the impression that he had the evening's activities organized and entirely under control. It would take all of forty minutes to shatter that illusion, but for now the façade held as Jarred Burdette introduced himself, the program, and the five panelists.

The questions had been designed to address the psycho-social needs of middle class African Americans and white liberals who portrayed King as their figurehead—preaching freedom for oppressed African Americans, while advocating non-violent means to achieve civil rights. King was "revolutionary" in a safe sort of way, according to this version of his life and teaching. Martin Luther King Day events like this were viewed by those who staged them as win-win situations in which everyone except the crazed racists got to walk away feeling righteous and justified. Liberal whites could pat themselves on the backs for sponsoring and supporting an event celebrating the quintessential Civil Rights leader, and middle class African Americans could safely take pride in an event reinforcing the comforting, though mendacious, message that America had purged itself of its racist past through the sacrificial offering of Martin Luther King.

Appropriately, the questions Jarred asked steered clear of issues like systemic racism, the shrinking black middle class, or the growing dissatisfaction among non-middle class blacks. Initially the focus would be on historical topics pertaining to King and the Civil Rights Movement: What was their significance? How do we experience their impact today? What things still need to be done? Jarred then brought the discussion into the present with questions addressed to the panelists such as: How do you see the spirit of Martin Luther King perpetuated in your roles as community leaders? Each panelist was allowed a few minutes to give a personal statement about King. Obviously this was designed to give the politically motivated among them (virtually all in one way or another) a chance to wax eloquently and plug shamelessly their various campaigns and projects. True to form, all took full advantage of the opportunity—except Willie Lightfoot, who did not partake in this self-promotion and whose responses to the questions posed seemed to obscure the agenda of the evening.

As Jarred wrapped up the first part of the program by summarizing the messages as he had heard them from the panelists, a tense feeling of anticipation began to well up inside me. I could see stagehands performing last minute tests on the audience microphone at the head of the isle to the right of the stage, and Sr. Grace was out of her seat bobbing up and down like a nervous squirrel eating nuts—giving encouragement and answering questions. Amazingly, no one noticed her. No one noticed the 60 people who had arrived by bus from the House of Mercy. No one noticed their nervous energy and group consciousness. Soon their inattention would be rewarded.

With an affectionate smile out of the corner of his mouth, C.W. nudged me saying, "Gracie is only making them more nervous. She just can't leave well enough alone."

I smiled back and gave him a reaffirming nod of my head.

The microphones were ready, the house lights rose and Jarred announced that the panelists would be taking questions from the audience.

"Let the games begin!" I intoned in a hushed voice.

"Amen!" C.W. chuckled knowingly.

Immediately a platoon of about ten from the House of Mercy broke ranks and clamored for a place in line. This eager crew was eventually followed by individuals who were intermittently dispatched from the congregation, which would soon double as not only a source of speakers, but also a cheering section for those at the microphone. The organizers looked puzzled and annoyed by this overwhelming response to the request for questions. Technical crewmembers rushed to reorganize themselves into ushers and crowd control personnel.

The Organizers had rehearsed a few polite questions with two family members of station personnel. These two had been standing at the microphones for about five minutes and now they were given their cue. Their questions were general, much like those Jarred had been asking throughout the program. Given the way these questions were lifelessly read off index cards, the questioners obviously could take little ownership of the perspectives that lay behind them. The perfunctory answers from the panelists indicated the questions came as no surprise. The contrived nature of the entire event was never clearer.

C.W. and I rose to our feet simultaneously as the polite questioning ended and the main event began. Greg was the first to the microphone. Flush with adrenaline and emboldened by his companions' supportive cheers, his customary lack of confidence would not be an issue this night. He began the rhetorical questioning outlining his personal struggles with racism, but he would eventually address the concerns of all his brothers and sisters. Like God answering Job, Greg recited a litany of offences that unto themselves spoke eloquently of the fundamental racism and classism at the heart of American society.

> *I am a young black man who is strong!*
> *Who is intelligent!*
> *Who has skills and talents!*
> *Who has an education and who has proven his worth*
>   *on the job!*
> *I am trustworthy and I get along with my coworkers!*
> *Yet I have struggled all my life to find decent*
>   *employment in this town and across this state!*
> *I live between poor paying part time jobs,*
>   *unemployment, welfare and the street!*
> *And I am not alone!*
> *There is a whole city out there filled with young men*
>   *and women just like me!*

> *Where were YOU leaders of the black community when a white rookie foreman fired me, the ONLY black man in his work group, his first day on the job?!*
>
> *Where were you when they forced me to take demeaning classes in how to fill out job applications at the unemployment office?!*
>
> *Where were you when I stood in line all day only to be humiliated by jaded workers at the welfare office?!*
>
> *Where were you when my landlord threw me out on the street because welfare sent my check to the wrong address and then would not reinstate me because I had no permanent residence?!*
>
> *What would Martin Luther King have to say about that?!*
>
> *What would he believe and who would he stand with?!*
>
> *Where is the justice for us?!*
>
> *Who dreams a dream for us?!*

That night Greg would be a confident prophet. Prince would speak his mind clearly. Tricky Dick would tell it like it was, and Mrs. Washington would be silent no more. Fifteen minutes after the event ended, and long after most of the panelists had walked away in disgust, House of Mercy guests were still coming forward to the microphone.

As I surveyed the panic-stricken and dumbfounded faces of the stagehands—unable to act without appearing reactionary on local television—I realized that what Grace had prophesied earlier in the evening had all come true. Indeed, the margins had erupted at the center, and neither would be quite the same for the experience. For 15 minutes on that cold, mid-January night, the illusions of the *status quo* were shattered. In a *Matrix* moment of fleeting awareness the voices of the disaffected were heard. That night I had a vision of God laughing and cheering, waiving her big black arms over her head, dancing ecstatically, celebrating a victory in heaven mirrored here on earth. In a small way, the lowly had been raised as the comfortable squirmed on their living room couches. God looked upon all that had transpired, and she was glad indeed. And when God was finished dancing, she raised her fist and cried, "*Carpe Diem.*"

The Upper Room

A day spent entertaining and supervising a dozen disabled adults with a median developmental level somewhere in the toddler range demanded a very special kind of end-of-day ritual in order to thoroughly unwind. For me, it required rigorous physical exercise, a big meal and lots of mind numbing television to fully expunge the hours of childish activities that had been rehearsed so many times before with the same group of individuals who were pathetically and perpetually trapped at a very early stage of intellectual, psychological and social development. Throughout my years of graduate studies I had worked in various capacities with the developmentally disabled. Just a few months before, I had successfully defended my doctoral dissertation on John Courtney Murray; nonetheless, these days found me changing diapers at the Crittenden Day Treatment Center in Henrietta, NY, with evenings devoted sporadically to adjunct teaching for St. Bernard's Institute. The countless applications I sent out to any and every college and university seeking to fill a teaching position in religious ethics yielded nothing more than a couple of stray perfunctory interviews at institutions that were clearly very interested in other candidates. It was obvious that if I was going to put my education to good use it was going to have to happen outside the traditional confines of academia.

That opportunity would arrive the day following Martin Luther King Day in 1994 when I received a phone call from Sr. Grace who wanted to 'unpack' our experience from the night before. The call interrupted the second in a pair of back-to-back dinnertime episodes of the Simpson's. As Bart tortured Homer on TV, Grace invited me to join her in what would become a long-term adventure.

"Can you come over to meet with us about last night?" Grace asked.

"Sure. What's up?" I wondered, thinking maybe something had happened after the event that I hadn't witnessed.

"Oh nothing…and everything. A lot of people are excited around here about our success last night and I want to capitalize on the momentum we've generated," said Grace, sounding like a reincarnated Saul Alinsky.

"That's a great idea. How do I fit in?" I said, still equivocal about what I wanted more: a cold, but interesting night out at the House of Mercy, or a warm, though pointless night in, around the television.

"Tom, I know you're busy with your full time job and your part time teaching at St. Bernard's, so feel free to say no, but we were wondering if you might hold some classes here at the House of Mercy and teach everyone here how to be radical," Grace said in her usual understated hyperbole. As I pondered what Grace would expect of a "radical" curriculum she continued:

"You have so much knowledge and experience regarding protest and community organization I thought you might be willing to share it with all the staff here—especially after our success last night. Wasn't that great?"

"Uh…yeah. Of course." I said, responding to her rhetorical query about last night. Grace immediately took that as an affirmation of her entire plan, so she quickly fell upon the dying carcass of my post-Crittenden ennui, and enlisted me as the instructor in what would become a "radical" school for us all.

"Fantastic! See you about eight in the Upper Room?" she concluded with an inadvertent biblical allusion.

"OK." I said, as I hung up, still trying to determine at what point, if any, in the previous exchange I had made a decision for myself to venture out for the second cold January night in a row. Grace had the momentum of a tractor trailer traveling at high speed—the rest of us often found ourselves sucked into her vortex, never entirely sure whether our actions were voluntary or compulsory. Most of the time I spent at the House of Mercy felt as though it was sustained by this odd mixture of compulsion and volition.

Grace had completely overestimated my qualifications to act as "professor" in this school for budding "radicals." My knowledge of protest and community organization was heavily weighed in favor of the theoretical. My experience, at this stage, could easily be summed up in a few sentences. I had been peripherally involved in anti-war and anti-nuclear protests throughout my years in college and graduate school—never functioning as an organizer of these events, though I did serve on the organizing committee for a local Pax Christi for a few years in the early 1990's. And I had lived in Chicago for a year where I experienced marginal exposure to the Woodlawn Organization, while residing in the poor Southside neighborhood of Englewood as I pursued a Masters of Divinity at Catholic Theological Union.

On the other hand, the educational column of my "radical" resume was generally more impressive. I held an M.A. from St. Bernard's Institute in Rochester, NY and a Ph.D. from the University of St. Michael's College in Toronto, both in social ethics. My areas of expertise included liberation theologies, and fortunately, my mentors in both graduate programs, Marvin Mich and Lee Cormie, were veterans of various reform movements. Both were also outstanding proponents of a radical understanding of the ethical task—one that actively included the poor and marginalized in the process of social transformation. Little did I know that the House of Mercy was about to become a laboratory where these theories would have ample opportunity to prove their relative worth.

As I cleared off the dinner table and started the evening dishes I began to organize my thought for the task ahead. I wondered how well the relatively esoteric economic, political, social and theological notions in my head would translate into a setting occupied by so many individuals who had not even completed high school. I worried about whether they would find me boring, or worse, merely academic. The more I ruminated on this anticipated mismatch, the more unenthusiastic I became about my role that evening. General gloom had set in when, in a graced moment of uncharacteristic clarity, it dawned on me that the focus of the evening should not be *my* impressions and interpretations, but *theirs:* those of the guests at the House of Mercy. With this new conception of the evening's plan my morale improved palpably. I wasn't too keen on hearing myself lecture, but I was very interested in gaining some insight into the ways this group of people made sense of their social world. Maybe my theories and their experiences would cross-pollinate and bear fruit in some, as yet, unforeseen way.

The distance between my house on the Southeast side of the city and the House of Mercy located on the near North side was such that my car's heating system would just begin to make the cab comfortable as I arrived at my respective destination. During the winter months I normally spent the first fifteen minutes of almost every car trip alternating between driving tasks and defogging or deicing the windshield. The first few minutes were often spent in a contorted posture attempting to maximize the field of vision offered by a grapefruit-sized patch of the windshield that lay directly beneath the defrost vent. My no-frills, subcompact Subaru wagon was quirky—like a mongrel, stray dog, who becomes a beloved family pet—but it always got me to the place I wanted to go. It also inspired some of my most creative apologetics.

As I approached the House of Mercy I could see only the glow of the interior lights casting rectangular spotlights on the snow banks surrounding each side of the buildings. The sunken front room had no windows so on my headlong approach to the building it disappeared into the blackness of the night as its silhouetted outline was framed by the shimmering snow banks. Unlike the night before, there were only a few cars in the driveway, which left just enough room for me to tuck in the back end of my car out of the path of oncoming traffic. There were no people conversing and milling around outside as there had been the night before, and when I pushed the front door open there were only three people sitting in the sunken room. Last night I had seen this room packed with as many as 20 times that number. For a moment, I stood in that room silently absorbing an entirely pristine experience of the House of Mercy—one that felt calm, familiar, and home-like.

"Hey there teach', how you doin'?" Proclaimed a loud and clear voice that startled me. As I turned to respond to the query that seemed to be directed at me, a short black woman, about 5 feet tall, was approaching with a pronounced limp that had an odd dance-like rhythm. Her big smile made me feel welcome and I vaguely remembered our brief introduction the night before as we were standing in the TV studio hallway with C.W. and Grace. I wanted to greet her by her name, but the only one that came to mind as I held out my hand was Mary Ann, which I knew was wrong somehow.

"Hi, how's it goin'?" I said flashing my own big smile in response.

She looked at my outstretched hand and chortled,

"Put that thing away an' gimme' a hug!" With that she threw her arms around me, locking me in an embrace that was surprisingly hearty for a woman of her stature. While still in her embrace I detected an unusual odor which would later be identified as a mixture of cheap wine and crack. The "Mary Jane Mixer" normally preserved its namesake in a functional state of euphoria that somehow fit her role at the House of Mercy.

With a knowing smile she brought my fruitless guessing to a close.

"The name's Mary Jane, and I'm known around here as the hostess with the mostest." She delivered the last half of this introduction with great glee and gusto, punctuating the words "hostess" and mostest" by swinging her arms over her head and thrusting her hips first to the right and then to the left. It was a delightful gesture and for a brief moment I had a flashback to my vision of God the night before. I was certain God would be flattered by the spontaneous simile.

She completed her introduction with a slow deep-throated laugh. Turning away and motioning up the short flight of stairs with her hand she said, "Follow me, the others are upstairs."

We passed through the same hallway I had traveled the night before on my way to Grace's office, and there, again, was a lucklessly devoted crowd of viewers mesmerized by Vanna White's ability to turn a letter, and Pat Sajack's wheel spinning. Apparently accustomed to intermittent bodies passing before the shrine, the faithful stoically maintained their holy gaze.

Instead of veering right and heading into Grace's office, Mary Jane led me on a winding path through the kitchen to the back of the house and up a steep, cluttered and narrow stairway to the second floor of the building. We had to duck a few times on the way up. At the top, a banister with a handrail leaning at an angle gave the scene a Salvadore Dali character. When I grabbed the rail for stability it swung precariously back in the other direction only heightening the carnival funhouse character. At the top of the stairs were some offices crammed full of boxes brimming with various household items like paper towels, toilet paper and bath accessories. As we walked back towards the front of the house we finally came to the "Upper Room." Behind the door I could hear the familiar sounds of chatting, laughing, and furniture being moved. I reached to knock, but Mary Jane opened the door and pushed me into the room saying with her now familiar flair for the dramatic,

"Here he is everybody, signed, sealed and delivered."

"Thanks, Mary Jane," said Grace, and without missing a beat she embraced me and introduced me to everyone in the room. Meanwhile, Mary Jane excused herself in order to return to her hostess duties.

Like every other room at the House of Mercy, the Upper Room was a warehouse for various sundry items that could not find a home elsewhere—all of which had recently been bulldozed into an attic crawlspace or against the south wall for the sake of our meeting. Old computers covered with grade school textbooks, donated clothing, children's toys, a lamp laying on its side, a box of miscellaneous bits and pieces, some framed pictures of Civil Rights heroes, and two electric stove elements sat on a long desk surrounded on each side by chairs, boxes and stacks of other randomly arranged things. The floor was old, warn, unfinished decking, probably dating back one hundred years or more. It bowed inward from the walls toward the center of the room as if water needed to be drained to this center point, like a locker room shower stall. The only water that might need to be drained in this room would come from the leaky roof overhead which was only partially insulated against the cold Rochester winter.

I fumbled toward my seat around a long unfinished table made of plywood and sawhorses. Bare light bulb illumination cast harsh shadows against the walls and floors, making navigation around the backs of chairs more difficult. I could feel the coldness of the metal folding chair through my jeans as I sat to face a crowd that was about evenly divided between those I could name and those I couldn't. Since our initial introduction had been so cursory I asked everyone if we could go around the table once again and give our names and tell a little something about ourselves. I volunteered to be the first to perform this tedious, though useful preface to our meeting in order to give others a little time to collect their thoughts for their brief moment in the spotlight. After my introduction I turned to my left and suggested that we go in a circle around the table.

Sitting to my left was Sr. Rita Lewis, who was a Sister of Mercy, like Grace, and had joined Grace a few years after the House of Mercy was established in 1986. She was a small woman in her late 30's with long, earth-colored hair, usually styled in a neo-hippy fashion that seemed to fit so well with her personality. She wore plain clothes and drove a perpetually struggling, late 1970's era, AMC Hornet. Her face had a girlish appearance and she had an infectious smile that often accompanied her puckish laugh. Like the other three permanent staff members, she was a jack-of-all-trades, who frequently found herself doing multiple duties like distributing clothing and food while counseling a pregnant mother regarding both her good-for-nothing boyfriend as well as her financial status with social services. Sr. Rita multi-tasked all day long and well into the night, every day of the week, though she rarely showed signs of burning out, or even fringing at the edges. Her passion was informed by a thoroughly practical nature and those characteristics combined seamlessly in this uniquely steadfast servant of the poor.

Rita's introduction was modest, though confidently brief. She then passed the baton to Tricky Dick who was not prepared to offer us more than his name. Prince was next and he was eager to follow Tricky Dick's precedent for succinct introductions. Facing Prince on the other side of the table was a young African American man in his early 30's named Kevin. He had an average build on a six-foot frame and was clothed in a way that suggested he was not a homeless guest at the House of Mercy. He gave a more complete introduction, recounting an educational background that was witnessed by a substantive vocabulary couched in well-crafted sentences. His self-assured words and delivery were belied by his coy smile and downcast eyes. Unfortunately, his bold façade was transparent enough to even the casual observer, revealing a sensitive and timid side to his personality that could be, and often was, exploited by the mean streets and its inhabitants. Kevin was a genuinely kind person who would put his native intelligence and substantial energy to good use for the sake of the poor and homeless—even at those times when he wasn't given the appreciation he was due.

The next person in our clockwise course around the table was Greg, who waved shyly at me and then everyone else as he reminded us that we already knew him. Keen on escaping the limelight, Greg concluded his concise introduction by turning to his left, and with a tah-dah hand gesture, gave the floor up to Sr. Gloria. Like Sr. Rita, Sr. Gloria was one of the three Sisters of Mercy working at the House of Mercy. Sr. Gloria was as delicate as Grace was robust. Like Grace, Gloria liked to hug, but embracing Gloria was something that one negotiated with a considerable degree of care, given her smaller and lighter corpus. Gloria was a few years older than her cousin Grace, which placed her somewhere in her late 50's or early 60's. She had short, dark hair peppered with a dash of gray that was topped off by the traditional headdress of her order's habit. Except for this item, however, she did not wear the rest of the habit. That being said, she wore more of the habit than either Grace or Rita. Self-effacing to a vice, Gloria put remarkable amounts of energy into making herself inconspicuous. She busied herself with the smallest jobs she could find at the House of Mercy. Nothing, it seemed, was too insignificant in her estimation. She was an incarnation of all those sayings ascribed to Jesus concerning the "meek," the "poor in spirit," and the "least of these," and for this reason, Gloria was also one of the most transparent models of discipleship I had ever met. She was a long-suffering soul who had chosen to suffer along with the poorest of the poor.

After an agonizingly demure introduction, Gloria apologetically surrendered the floor to C.W. who sat to her left at the end of the table. C.W. perfunctorily introduced himself and then gave a succinct, though nonetheless moving testimonial of his experience as a homeless person, highlighting the role that the House of Mercy and Sr. Grace had played in his personal redemption. Apparently he became homeless after a failed marriage, and this situation was exacerbated by his addiction to alcohol. Eventually, he made his way to the House of Mercy, where, with Grace's assistance, he began to help himself by helping others who had found themselves in a similar predicament. He was now an indispensable part of the fabric at the House of Mercy—as essential to its spirit and operation as its founder.

With that, C.W. had, for all intents and purposes, introduced Grace who was sitting across the table from him and immediately to my right. Grace raised her hands and eyebrows and gave everyone a big smile saying,

"If you don't know me, then, what are you doing here?!"

Everyone laughed, some nodding and grunting knowingly. Grace then turned to me and confidently affirmed,

"They're all yours."

I laughed in response with a mixture of genuine mirth and a self-conscious sense of the absurdity of such a statement. I wasn't really sure why I was in this room with these people on this night. But, as I looked around the room at the various faces expressing similar sentiments of doubt and mild confusion, it occurred to me that we were more unified than I had first imagined. Everyone in that room had shared a singular experience the night before. Not only that, it had been experienced from a shared perspective since we had formed a group consciousness beforehand, traveled to the event together, supported one another, and now we were about to form an interpretive consensus—a hermeneutic as it would be known by some scholars.

"It is certainly flattering to think that you are all mine." I said, drawing a few titters from the assembly, "but it was not my intention to come here tonight and tell you what *I* believe and how *I* experience my world. In fact, probably most of you have had your fill of relative strangers invading your world, imposing themselves and their foreign perspectives on you, your family, your friends and associates."

A few surprised nods told me I was on the right track.

"You have all probably had experiences like that in school, at social service agencies, on the job, and in church. I know I have, and they tend to be frustrating and unfulfilling. I try to pay attention at first, but then

I loose interest and become apathetic."

"You got that right." Said Tricky Dick.

"Yeah, nobody listens to you when you're poor." Greg chimed in.

Everyone concurred as each of the nine people at the table had a chance to explain their experiences of frustration with traditional paternalistic models of administration and education. A litany of grievances began to emerge and I quickly scrambled for a pen and paper so I could record these lamentations. As I did so, the participants became even more vociferous and animated—watching as their every word was etched on my page. For some, this would be an experience of being taken seriously, perhaps for the first time in their lives.

While I performed my clerical role that evening I listened closely to each story acknowledging the pain, anxiety, fear, humor, and triumph embedded in the telling. As I listened, I realized I was the first obstacle that had to be overcome. My role as "teacher" had to be deconstructed, demythologized and drained of all of its toxic power to silence the "class" and trump all variant opinion. The assumptions that the black should listen while the white speak, and the poor be silent as the well-off expound, failed that night upon examination before a board of representatives at the House of Mercy. As we learned about each other and our collective struggles against imposed authorities, we learned even more about the way in which our gatherings would need to be organized. If we were ever going to address the inequality in our social systems with any degree of credibility, we would first need to honestly address the inequalities that existed among ourselves. That night we decided that I would not be telling the group what to think, how to speak their mind, or whether or not the rest of the group would have meaningful input into the process. My academic degree and I were a valued resource and would have an important, though limited, role to play in what would eventually become much more than a theological discussion group.

It took more than an hour to fully exorcise the demons of social standing, which use extrinsic standards to assign intrinsic value to certain opinions, while discounting other notions outright, based solely on the status of the deliverer. The effect of this exorcism on the group gathered in the "Upper Room" was remarkable. Those who had once been silent were now boldly speaking their minds. Those who had been slouching in disinterest were now attentive and on the edge of their seats. The room was abuzz with a new spirit and each of us began speaking with a new voice—one that could be heard, understood and valued in the presence of equals.

"I thought I wasn't goin' to understand a word you said." Prince said enthusiastically. "But I was wrong. I got everything you said as if you wuz Tricky Dick here, or C.W."

Everyone at the table seconded Prince's sentiment and I nodded my appreciation to those assembled. Then seeking opinions about the future direction of our little group (since we had never actually addressed the issue of the Martin Luther King Day action) I asked awkwardly,

"Well, what does this mean?"

After an extended silence, Rita quietly said,

"*Parousia.*"

Collision

I was really in no condition to be asked to wait so long on hold. The nauseating smell of refried breakfast grease had filled the breezeway of the blue-collar diner where I was trying to get a hold of my fellow workers from a pay phone to tell them I would be late for work that day. I had been on my way to work when an older gentleman on his way to morning Mass with his wife ever so slowly swerved his Toyota Camry into the path of oncoming southbound traffic. As I shifted lanes to avoid him, he continued to pull left into the lane I now occupied only a few yards behind. Quick reflexes saved his car from damage, but sent my Subaru and me twisting and screeching into the opposite lane. Just as I was about to come to a stop, the back end of my little wagon swung around, driver's side first, depositing my car perpendicularly across both lanes of northbound traffic, right in the path of a middle-aged woman in a domestic compact, who plowed into my back quarter panel, sending both cars spinning.

Only my comfortable sense of routine had been injured; however, when I got out of my car to assess the situation I found the woman who had run into my car in an apparent state of shock. The eyes of countless stressed-out commuters silently willed me out of existence as I tried to clear at least one lane in each direction. I felt like the evil antagonist in a live theatre production as I practiced my chaos management skills out on the street. My attention was drawn to the church parking lot where I watched as Mr. Magoo and his wife calmly parked their car a few hundred feet away and entered St. Ann's Church, oblivious to the chain reaction which they had set in motion moments ago.

In accord with the occasion, a morose employee from the funeral home across the street made the requisite calls for the police and ambulance. As fortune would have it, a young man driving behind me witnessed the accident and helped corroborate my telling of the incident to the police.

After getting knocked around like a rag doll, conscripted into *ad hoc* rescue work, questioned by police for half an hour, and waiting too long for the tow truck to arrive, I was nearing the limits of composure as I hung up the phone at the diner and redialed the number for my employer.

"Good morning, Crittenden Day Treatment Center, Donna speaking." Donna was our secretary whose advanced cerebral palsy did not dissuade her from this often demanding and under appreciated position at the center.

"Hi Donna. Tom again. No one picked up so I decided to hang up and call again." I said, trying to conceal the frustration I was feeling.

"Oh, sorry Tom. I think Peter is in a meeting. Do you want to speak to someone in the room?" The "room" to which she referred was a converted grade school classroom that was the activity center where two coworkers, a dozen developmentally disabled adults and I spent our weekdays.

"Sure, Donna. But before you transfer me I just want to tell you I've had a serious accident and I will be very late for work today because I have to go with the tow truck to the repair shop." I said, just in case I was cut off or placed in phone system limbo once again.

"Oh my God! Are you alright?" Donna exclaimed, sincerely concerned.

"I'm fine. Another person was injured. My car was totaled." I summarized the situation as laconically as I could because the tow truck had just pulled up to the accident scene.

"That's awful! I'm so sorry. Here, I'll transfer you to the room." Donna said, apparently sensing the renewed urgency of my situation. This time the transfer went through and after rehearsing the predictable sentiments of shock and condolences with Shelly and Jane, I was ready to end the conversation.

"Well, the tow truck man is here and I need to get out to my car because he seems to be looking for me." I said, sounding more rushed than I really was.

"OK Tom, take it easy. I hope you didn't have any other plans for the day." Shelly said, half joking.

I hung up as the realization was overtaking me—indeed, I did have other plans for the day. It was now late February 1994 and a few weeks earlier I had committed to a weekly Thursday night schedule with the group at the House of Mercy. But there was no time to call that morning and Grace wouldn't be in her office until 2:00pm anyway; so I scurried out to the accident scene and made towing arrangements with a surprisingly friendly tow truck operator.

I'm sure I saw dollar signs flash in the eyes of the tow truck operator when I told him I wanted my car taken to the dealership in a town 20 miles away. I was informed that their tardiness was due to the fact that they had to call upon the services of their only flatbed truck since my car was in such a bad state that it couldn't be towed. The operator tethered the front end of my car like a helpless bass on the end of a fisherman's line as he landed it on the deck of his flatbed truck. The only detail missing from this metaphorical stage was the final flip-flop struggle and the cooler full of ice. I gawked blankly from a distance as order was restored piece by piece to a small, but important stretch of this four lane, north-south arterial roadway. My car and I were the last to bid adieu to a recently chaotic and dangerous setting, which was both understandably repelling, yet also oddly alluring. Our safe daily routines tend to be both our salvation and our addiction. Their disruption frequently evokes a mixture of dread and liberation.

My response that day to sensory overload in the aftermath of my major collision was to tune reality out as much as possible and reflect on the events of the past month at the House of Mercy. We had met a total of five times in the Upper Room and we were beginning to refer to ourselves as the "forum," though various other less flattering labels were being bandied about among the downstairs crowd. Nevertheless, we were planning our first action using the community organizing principles of Saul Alinsky as our guide. Alinsky's first principle was to capture the interest of the people in the community by addressing a small and achievable goal. The community leaders were to treat this relatively small task as a great matter and should infuse the mission with powerful symbols that should be publicly expressed in the mass media.

Our first issue centered around a particularly dangerous traffic intersection in front of a public grade school near the House of Mercy that was without any signs or signals. A number of the neighborhood children had been injured at this intersection and one child had been killed during the last school year. In spite of its notorious reputation and its proximity to the grade school, the city had done nothing to rectify the situation. Our plan was to shame the city into placing a four way stop sign there and to hire morning and afternoon crossing guards.

Around the same time that the young black girl was killed at that intersection in question, a preschool-age white girl named Kali Poulton had been abducted in the suburbs. At our last meeting Kali came up as a topic in the midst of our discussion of the intersection and the death of the black schoolgirl. Our comparison of the way these two tragedies were reported by the media and mourned by the public would uncover for us another deformed feature on the racist landscape of America.

The story about the black girl appeared as a three-paragraph story in the B section of the daily issue of the local newspaper. No pictures of the girl or interviews with her parents ever appeared, either in print or on TV. Her tragic, negligent and untimely death went largely unnoticed in the greater Rochester metro area.

Meanwhile, the equally tragic abduction and murder of Kali Poulton was greeted with almost unparalleled fanfare. For the better part of a year one could not open a paper, turn on a news program, or even look at a bulletin board in Rochester without seeing the pageant photo of this blond Shirley Temple look-alike. Kali's parents were omnipresent teary-eyed guests on news broadcasts and talk shows desperately appealing to the public for information regarding her whereabouts. In white suburban America, it seems that the appetite for paranoid images of crime juxtaposed against smarmily distorted pictures of the "family," simply cannot be satiated. When the body was finally identified, it was laid to rest in near royal fashion, reprising in the media for our final satisfaction the teary-eyed parents and the beauty queen photos.

Every year black children are abducted in poorer neighborhoods of Rochester and few ever received even a tiny fraction of the attention that Kali's case attracted. Conversely, had Kali Poulton died at a notoriously dangerous intersection, which had been brought to the attention of City officials by parents time and again, it is certain her case would have received far more press than the black girl's death.

A cynic might have complained that Kali's case was all overdone *ad nauseum*. A hardened cynic might have even detected something peculiarly staged about the manipulative media coverage. However, the more critical sensibilities being formed in our "forum" would not bemoan Kali Poulton or her parents their rightful place in our public memories as symbols of something brutally tragic. The offense for us lay in the relatively nonchalant treatment of the black schoolgirl's death.

"She was a human being—a human being!" Prince proclaimed, punctuating the last two words by stabbing the table with his index finger then crossed his arms and turned in his seat away from the assembly. He was seeing clearly, maybe for the first time, the detailed mechanisms of a racist apparatus and he was simultaneously angry, insulted, indignant, and despondent. Far from setting him free, the truth had ambushed Prince in a bewildering swarm of unwelcome insights. For a moment, he had nothing to say, but had to say something, so before we could intrude with our corrections and condolences he lurched back into a forward position in his chair and punched at the silence with a few staccato negations.

"No...no...no...no...NO!" Prince bobbed up and down aggressively at the hips after each exclamation with his palms pressing ever more firmly on the table. Beginning with his left index finger pointed in the air and continuing with long sweeping gestures of his bony arm, he conducted our field of vision as he finally assembled his feelings into a coherent message.

"When we do this thing for her. When we get the city to come out here an' put up a stop sign. We don't jus' do it for her an' those kids. We do it for us. We sayin' she matters...those kids matter...an' all us black folks matter...jus' as much as you white folks!" His message reached its climax with his finger pointed directly at me. The uneasy impression that I was being identified as the archetypal representative of my race was confirmed as I sensed all eyes at the table were now firmly fixed on the target of his pointing finger. The ball had unexpectedly landed in my court and the forum was awaiting my response. This was a challenge no one had anticipated though anyone with any experience working in interracial settings could have predicted. This was a proving ground and my reaction to Prince's speech would determine my credibility with the members of the forum.

I paused momentarily, collecting my thoughts and composing a thoughtful response.

"Yes, indeed we need to 'raise up the lowly' in our efforts with the City on this issue. We believe on one level that we share a common humanity, but that is being contradicted and undermined constantly by racist social constructs. In this case, the obvious social construct, and often the first line of defense for structural racism, is the media. So yes, Prince, we do need to force the media and the City to revisit the humanity of the black girl and all black children when we confront these issues with them. If we don't, I think we miss an important opportunity to challenge the broader racist culture."

As I spoke I could see the impact my words were having on the group, which had so recently found itself on the razor's edge. Many were slumping back into more relaxed postures, worried expressions were softening and a few flashed smiling nods telling me I was prescribing the right kind of medicine for our collective nervous disorder.

"But, as Mary's words in Luke's Gospel tell us, every 'raising of the lowly' needs to coincide with a 'casting down of the rulers.' These are often trickier waters to navigate because, while it is a difficult struggle to get all people to agree that everyone has equal dignity, it is a truly monumental task to convince the proud and the mighty that their estimation of themselves and their kinfolk is too high. However, I would claim that we need to do both 'raising' and 'lowering' if we are ever going to achieve the kind of balance and harmony in society that are genuine signs of true justice."

The relaxation that had recently followed upon the growing anxiety in the forum was now giving way to thoughtful pensive expressions. After the brief test a moment ago, which I apparently passed, the forum had restored itself to its normal state of active inquiry, barely skipping a beat.

"So what does all this mean in our case?" Kevin asked, fingering his chin with his right hand in a thoughtful manner.

"I mean, how do we restore balance by 'casting down' the high and mighty?" He continued. "We know we need to retell the story of the black girl who was killed, so that, this time, everyone hears and takes notice. But I just don't know what we can do to 'cast down' the mighty in this case."

The group seconded Kevin's sentiments and a number of spontaneous conversations began to break out between members sitting next to one another. After a few seconds of chaotic discussion C.W. brought the forum back to order.

"Hey, hey, hey!" He shouted, silence following the third exclamation. "Let's keep it together and make this thing productive for everyone." He said, leaning forward in his seat with his chest looming over the table. He then turned to me asking pointedly:

"How would you answer that Tom?"

This was my second major challenge of the evening, but this time it wasn't my character that was being challenged, but my knowledge, understanding and creativity. I had to admit:

"I'm not really sure C.W., Kevin's question is an excellent one. It seems clear to me that we need to reaffirm the humanity of the dead black girl by invoking her powerful memory—just as Prince suggested. But I think we also need to reflect back to the people of Rochester the media's distorted image of humanity in its exclusive, sensationalized and disproportionate treatment of the Kali Poulton case. This is a far more delicate task since we run the very real risk of losing credibility by being labeled heartless, envious and possibly even friends of murderers and criminals. My question to the rest of the group is: should we risk losing credibility during our first public action by attempting to address both aspects of this racist ideology? If so, then how can we best get our message across so our beliefs are not turned against us through clever rewording and selective quoting?"

We never achieved consensus on that question that evening, but the forum had taken enormous strides forward. My own credibility had reached new heights as could be witnessed by the familiar way in which the members of the forum began to treat me after the meeting. We talked, laughed and shared revealing stories until the wee hours of the morning. That night set a precedent for future meetings in which the forum would evolve away from a classroom setting towards a more and more loosely structured gathering. Eventually the forum would become as much a support group as it was a classroom, as much a social hour as it was an organized body, and as much a party as it was a political movement.

I was deep in reflection concerning all of these things when the mechanic's voice drew me out of my head.

"Mr. O'Brien!" He emphasized, probably for the third or fourth time.

"Yes, oh sorry. I was lost in thought. What is it?" I mumbled hurriedly, trying to bring myself back into the present. The mechanic continued:

"We estimate repairs on your vehicle will take more than three weeks. Do you have a ride back to the City?"

"Uh, yeah, the tow truck driver said he would take me back to the City. Any idea how much it will cost?" I said as I collected my things.

"We have to wait to get an estimate from your insurance agent. They might just total your car and pay you the replacement cost. There was some structural damage that might cost more to fix than replace," the mechanic informed me with his chin in his chest, writing down something on a form attached to his clipboard.

"Here, please sign at the bottom. This gives us authorization to proceed with any and all necessary repairs. In these kinds of cases receiving owner permission to repair every little thing is simply impossible," he said, handing me the clipboard and pen.

"Yeah, it is a mess isn't it?" I said, more to myself than to the mechanic, as I scrawled my name on the bottom of the form. I thought about the practical aspects of being car-less for three weeks and it felt oddly exhilarating. Part of this feeling came from the brainteaser, problem solving, aspect of imagining various solutions to the question of how I would get from one place to another without a car. Part of it came from the sense of adventure that came over me when I thought about riding the awkward and inefficient public transportation system, or walking along the river bike path. However, the most satisfying aspect of being car-less came from my general distaste for driving automobiles—one of the most environmentally disastrous technologies on the planet. What if they did total my car? Would I buy another one? Or, could I get by just fine without it? On the ride back into the City I dreamed of a morally elevated, temporarily car-free future in which I thumbed my nose at automobile commuters with an air of emancipation and just a touch of superiority. No longer weighed down by the mundane drudgery of negotiating traffic, or isolated from my natural environment, or entombed in an artificial projectile, I could turn my various journeys into physical and mental quests.

I called the House of Mercy from work that afternoon to update them on my situation and to inform them that I couldn't be with the forum that evening.

"Yeah?" A man answered abruptly at the House of Mercy. It sounded like Prince, but I wasn't sure.

"Hi, could I speak to Sister Grace please?" I said, using the same phone manners I had rehearsed with my mother as a five year old.

Without acknowledging my request the person behind the Prince-like voice at the other end dropped the receiver and started yelling in the background:

"Grace...? Gracie...? Sister Grace!!! (pause)...C.W.!"

"Yeah" Replied C.W.

"Tell Gracie there's a guy on the phone for her." Said the Prince-like receptionist.

"Who is it?" Requested C.W.

With that I heard the muffled sound of fumbling and then the sharper sounds of the phone receiver being picked up.

"Who dis'?" Asked the receptionist.

"This is Tom O'Brien." I introduced myself in a demeanor again taken from my Miss Manners training as a child.

"Oh hey! Tom, what's up?" Said the voice that I was now certain belonged to Prince.

"I'm fine, is this Prince?" I asked, taking a shot at identifying my phone partner.

"Yeah, hang on, I'll get Gracie." With that Prince again dropped the receiver and said to C.W.

"It's Tom."

"Tom who?" C.W. emphasized with mounting frustration.

"Yah know, Tom the teach," Prince announced mirthfully.

C.W. mumbled something and walked off into another room calling Grace's name. Prince picked up the receiver and said,

"You still there?"

"Yup." I said, in an uninspired voice.

"Grace'll pick up in a second." Prince muttered as he dangled the receiver by his index finger and thumb next to his ear just waiting for the chance to hang up and be rid of this ornery task. A few seconds passed before Grace came on the line.

"Good afternoon, Sister Grace speaking." She said as the click of Prince hanging up sounded in the background.

"Hi Grace, it's Tom O'Brien," I said, a little relieved to finally be connected to the right party.

"Oh, hi Tom, how's it going?" Grace's enthusiasm seemed to increase when she spoke to me. It was a very welcoming gesture.

"I'm fine, but I don't think I'll be able to make it to the forum tonight because I totaled my car on the way to work this morning." Grace, of course, was duly shocked by this news of mine and we rehashed in detail the events of the morning. However, she wasn't about to let me off the hook that easily.

"You should come tonight. We have a big surprise for you. I think Rita will be in your part of town this evening. Sweet Thing is in the hospital again and Rita will be visiting him. She can pick you up on her way back to the House of Mercy." With that, my fast track to pedestrian utopia had been derailed.

I wondered what the big surprise might be. I knew Greg and Kevin had been working together independently of the rest of the forum on a project related to the proposed stop sign at the intersection near the grade school. I hadn't seen anything in the paper, but I usually paid only cursory attention to the local news and the editorials, so I could have easily missed the big surprise. Then again, if it had already hit the news, Grace probably wouldn't have billed it as a "big surprise."

I simply couldn't resist the lure of the unknown.

"OK, I'll see you tonight. When will Rita pick me up?"

"Oh around 7:30…maybe 8:00." Grace said, a little unsure herself. C.W. once informed me that Grace tended to work on "CP time"—colored people time—which was defined for me as a very imprecise and normally late schedule. According to my observations, the entire House of Mercy ran on CP time, and I would not be disappointed that evening as Rita pulled into my driveway around 8:15. I would never fully adjust to CP time and that night was no exception. I had been waiting promptly in my front room since 7:30, ready to scamper out to Rita's car at a moment's notice as though I were on assignment with Mission Impossible and this trip to the House of Mercy was some kind of precision assault. I would eventually loosen up a little bit—but not much. To my credit, I did very little complaining.

After bidding adieu to Miss Cat, my female tabby who had adopted me a few years back when I lived in Toronto, I slipped behind Tricky Dick into Rita's back seat where I shared space with three-ring binders, files, clothing and other things that couldn't be identified in the dark. When greetings and well wishes were finished, Rita and Tricky Dick returned to a conversation that had been interrupted momentarily by my retrieval. Rita was a no-nonsense type of driver who knew how to get from one place to another quickly and efficiently. I learned a new route from my house to the House of Mercy that night which would shave a couple of minutes off my usual commute.

Before we started our forum meeting I was compelled to recount, in detail, my harrowing accident and its aftermath. I was already growing weary of the telling and was beginning to gloss over the minutia and truncate inessential tidbits in an attempt to formulate a modest summary that could be told in five minutes or less. Unfortunately, the forum was an inquisitive crowd and those details that had been neglected in the digest version were to come to light under cross-examination. I ended the tale by telling everyone how good it felt to be without my car for three weeks. I could tell by the looks on their faces that few could relate to the sense of freedom I was experiencing over the loss of my car. After a short silence, Tricky Dick chuckled,

"You really takin' dis' homeless shit too seriously."

Everybody had a hearty laugh, which was a good way to start. The big surprise that Sr. Grace had tempted me with on the phone turned out to be a letter to the editor drafted by Greg and Kevin. They had been collaborating on the project since our last meeting when we discussed Kali Poulton and the dead black girl. Greg recited the letter like he was preaching a revival, and most of the forum responded in kind, shouting "amen" and other forms of exclamatory encouragement. After Greg's triumphant conclusion, it was Kevin's turn to inject his more restrained and studious interpretation of the letter and its process of composition. Our first product impressed us all; however, some of us knew it would need editing and refinement before the local newspaper would consider it for publication.

More than any previous forum gathering, that night we *worked* well into the wee hours of the next morning. We brainstormed, bickered and bargained our way through each word and phrase until we emerged at the other end of these negotiations staring bleary eyed and silently at a product that was virtually unchanged from the one that had been read to us four hours earlier. A few words had changed and some curt expressions softened, but the essence of the message remained. The only difference would be that now *their* message had become *ours,* and when Greg and Kevin delivered their editorial, they would speak for all of us in our stead.

There were a number of opinions in the group about the anticipated reaction this letter would elicit. Some believed it would shake people up and incite an angry response. Some thought it might be the starting point for a fruitful dialogue about this and other related issues. Others believed the letter was so convincing that the City would be forced by popular demand to admit the righteousness of our cause and erect the stop signs. I believed that editorials were a waste of time and that this would be, at best, a first step in a long arduous battle. It turned out that everyone was right—except me.

The editorial was hand delivered to the *Democrat & Chronicle* the next day by Kevin. A few days later, Greg and Kevin received notice that the letter would be printed and the Editor requested their pictures. The following Sunday edition ran the piece with the pictures of Kevin and Greg in a sidebar. It was the banner editorial displayed in larger type and prominently positioned on the page, and it became the immediate focus of attention both inside and outside the walls of the House of Mercy. Our next forum meeting was naturally absorbed by the excitement generated by the notoriety that two of our members had gained in our very first public action. Throughout the week Kevin and Greg had been interviewed by a wide array of local media and government celebrities. They had tweaked the conscience of a significant sector of the City of Rochester and were emerging from the streets as "experts" on this issue. It was a heady moment for both Greg and Kevin and their self-assured façade could never completely cloak the jumble of uncertain emotions that came with this unexplored territory. Nonetheless, they made us all proud, and represented our perspective on this issue forcefully and articulately. Kevin and Greg were black, poor, undereducated products of the street who responded to the call of their conscience when they became aware of an injustice in their midst. In the course of a few weeks, and as a result of a couple of hundred words, Greg and Kevin had stepped forward as the representatives, the prophets, and the voice of the people on the streets.

The next day the deadly intersection was resurrected into a four-way stop complete with crossing guards hired for morning and afternoon duties at the grade school. I was certainly very happy with the outcome, but there was a part of me that was a little deflated by the utter lack of resistance. I was also still embarrassed I had told everyone that editorial letters were a waste of time. Personal feelings aside, our first public action had achieved everything it was supposed to according to the theories of Saul Alinsky. It was a concern of the people on the street. It was an achievable objective. It was planned and spearheaded by the people themselves, and in the end, it was entirely their victory. An ardent spirit grew a hundred fold at the House of Mercy that day, and the forum would harvest that crop.

The forum had endured its first minor collision with the oppressive daily routine of American class elitism and racism, and they walked away in better shape than when they began. For now, they celebrated, but just around the corner lay a highway jammed with bigger, meaner targets stretching to the horizon. *Misere re nobis.*

On Stage

      I sat in the large multipurpose recreation room at Crittenden Day Treatment Center tuning my guitar while my new coworkers, Amy and Rebecca, set up folding chairs for my slowly accruing audience. Once a week on a Friday afternoon I led the entire Center in a camp style sing-along, which served the purposes of both clients and staff so well that it had become something of a tradition over the past few months. By Friday afternoon, burned out staff and hyperactive clients mingled into the makings of a volatile cocktail that demanded some form of dilution lest the cathartic forces of one or the other simmer into a real boilermaker. The Friday afternoon sing-alongs had become universally cherished by the clients, who enjoyed getting out of their rooms to sing; the staff, who enjoyed a good one hour break from intensive personal care; and the administration, who could count this as another one of *their* great ideas in spite of their near perfect lack of involvement in either its initiation, planning or perpetuation. Our administration would call our Friday afternoon gatherings a "win-win solution." These born again cheerleaders for Total Quality Management were fond of pointing out the imaginary silver lining around every category six tornado.

      "Doo-Dah." Came the familiar request from Dan, a client who suffered from mental retardation and a severe form of cerebral palsy that confined him to a wheelchair. I played along teasing him as I always did.

"No, I don't think we'll be singing that song today Dan. I don't think I remember how to play it."

Doooo-Daaaah!" Dan writhed in his chair, emphasizing his request for Camptown Races, his very favorite song, ever, in the whole wide world. I continued the game.

"Nope, the President of the United States just called reminding me there is a world-wide ban on singing the song Doo-Dah." With that Dan grabbed my *Rise Up Singing* songbook, holding it open, pointing randomly to the exposed pages, repeating his mantra:

"Doo-Dah." Barb, one of the staff members in his room intervened, removing the book from Dan's lap, flashing me a naughty-boy smile as she turned to reassure Dan:

"Is bad old Tom teasing you?" Barb asked playfully.

"Yeah." Dan said, confirming my guilt.

"Well if he doesn't sing Doo-Dah we'll just have to kick him afterwards. OK?" Barb said.

"Yeah." Dan agreed to the plan.

Knowing they were only half joking, I inserted Camptown Races near the end of the program and continued my preparations for the sing-along. The program included a variety of children's songs by the likes of Raffi, as well as some more tolerable folk and pop tunes like La Bamba and Proud Mary. We always finished off with a rousing rendition of the Happy Wanderer, normally preceded by Camptown Races, Dan's magical musical panacea. Our sing-along functioned like a concluding punctuation mark to our weeklong drama at Crittenden. When I was done, we all were done—everyone and everything got packed up, put away, and shipped off to another location. However, this week the sing-along would function more as an overture than a conclusion for me since I would be spending the weekend at the House of Mercy.

This particular ending to our workweek was more of the beginning of the end for me at Crittenden. Anxiety, regret, anticipation and relief came together in an unexpectedly ambivalent moment as I handed my resignation to my supervisor that morning. My work at Crittenden had become bleak and unfulfilling, yet real attachments to clients and staff had certainly developed. And although the paycheck was small, it was nonetheless regular and the benefits package was decent. The night before Sr. Grace informed me that an anonymous donor had given her $3,000 to use as she wished, and that she wished to hire me—at least for the summer—at $300 per week. I would receive cash and no benefits and I would get paid under the table since placing me on the payroll would somehow create tensions with the Sisters of Mercy mother house. Before Grace could finish her proposal I was composing the resignation letter in my head. Even if the employment was only temporary, this was the most exciting offer I had ever received. It was, first of all, a chance to experience in a very direct way the daily circumstances of the poorest of the poor in a modest sized North American city. It was also a chance to form my largely theoretical social beliefs—which I had spent more than a dozen years and countless dollars developing—into a coherent vision. How could I turn her down?

Although there were two weeks left in my contract, I pulled out of the Crittenden parking lot that night feeling like a long dreary and monotonous chapter in my life was coming to an end. Like someone driving through the seemingly endless Iowa cornfields in late August, I was ready for some fresh scenery. Even change for its own sake would be welcome; but in this case, it was clearly change for something better.

Big changes were on the horizon for the House of Mercy as well. Increasing demand for its services and regular controversial public exposure over the past few months combined to give the House of Mercy a priority status among some very influential forces. On the one hand, we were saying things that no one who was counted among the powerful wanted us to say. Therefore, there was an undercurrent in these discussions about ways to stop or silence us. On the other hand, we were a private religious organization doing a social service, and that was a perfect fit for traditional *laissez faire* ideology, which maintains that the government should play a minimal role in society. The question, therefore, became not an either-or decision, i.e., to do away with the House of Mercy or allow it to continue as it existed—the question evolved in more sophisticated directions—i.e., how to support the mission, while co-opting the message? We couldn't be aware of it at this juncture in our history, but the next few years would be marked by successive carrot and stick maneuvers by those with political and financial means.

That week Sr. Mary Jo Pierce, the provincial for the Sisters of Mercy in Rochester and a vocal opponent of Sr. Grace and the House of Mercy had unexpectedly and uncharacteristically offered to purchase and renovate a much larger building for the House of Mercy. The reason given for this apparent change of heart and unprecedented largess was that the City wanted to condemn and demolish the present location, yet "we" all wanted to preserve the good work being done there. These sentiments were suspicious coming from a woman who had so recently referred to the House of Mercy as an embarrassment. Nonetheless, larger digs was the first item on our wish list, and an offer like this couldn't be happening at a better time given the recent substantial increase in demand for our services. C.W. was especially fond of the idea of moving into a renovated space since he was in charge of maintaining the current dilapidated facility. A big juicy carrot dangled within our reach. We suspected there might be unseen strings attached, but we knew it was our destiny to seize this opportunity, come what may. On both accounts, we would not be disappointed.

Tonight, however, we wouldn't be discussing the feasibility of a new location or its impact on the current community of guests. We had spent so much time on this issue over the past few weeks that Grace asked us to hold a special meeting dedicated to the recent public attacks by Republican legislators leveled against the so-called welfare queens and teenage mothers. These characterizations of women on welfare came scripted for local conservative legislators from the national Republican headquarters. The interests of the wealthy elite were being served by redirecting, or more accurately, misdirecting middle-class and working-class frustration over stagnant wages and corporate downsizing toward the poor, who were themselves enjoying historically small pieces of the American pie. In this economy the rich and the poor were both on the move—each becoming more of what they already were. But the real incomes for the middle and working classes were stagnating for the most part, both showing slight but progressive depreciation over the past two decades.

The meeting began with Sr. Grace announcing my decision to accept her offer to join the House of Mercy staff.

"OK everybody, listen up. I have an announcement to make," she said in a loud voice knocking on the table with her fist to bring the room to order.

"Starting in a couple of weeks we will have a new staff member joining our team here at the House of Mercy." Everyone looked surprised, even C.W., Gloria and Rita. Obviously, Grace had kept this a very close secret. All at once, a number of people began to speak, each with a puzzled look and all with the same question on their minds. Out of the clamor rose C.W.'s voice:

"Well, are you going to make us guess?"

"It's Tom!" Grace exclaimed, looking at me with the proud smile of an Italian mother at her son's graduation.

Cheers, kudos and congratulations followed with handshakes, back slaps and even high fives from Kevin and Greg. I felt like I had just won the Daytona 500 and half expected a bottle of champagne and a huge vulgar trophy to appear at the doorway with a humongous novelty check made out to me for $3,000. Instead we consumed donated soda and chips, toasting my delivery from death to life with flat Sprite and warm Diet Coke. I had much to be thankful for that evening and this *ad hoc* eucharistic gathering would be repeated again and again over the next few years, each time commemorating for me this decisive leap of faith.

When the revelry died down, Grace began the meeting.

"OK, let's get down to business. We need a plan for Tuesday night's County Legislature Meeting." The House of Mercy had sent a busload of people to the last two County Legislature meetings at the invitation of one of the more liberal members, Bill Benet. He had wanted individuals to give witness to the plight of the poor in Rochester during the part of the meeting when members of the community at large could briefly bring their concerns before the legislators. Instead, it was the House of Mercy that would bear witness to a callous and denigrating attitude toward the poor, especially poor single mothers. At this County Legislature meeting the House of Mercy was going to give witness, but not to their poverty and poor living conditions. This time they would give witness to their anger and disgust for those legislators who had grown too comfortable and self-righteous to recognize the dignity and worth of the poor.

"We gotta' do somethin' different than what we done las' time. That jus' ain't gonna do," Prince interjected, chuckling through the last sentence in disgust.

"You got that right," seconded Tricky Dick. I hadn't made it to the last meeting so I asked:

"What did we do at the last meeting? Can anyone give me an idea of what happened and why we think something more needs to be done?"

Greg chimed in.

"For the most part, we just sat there and listened while these blowhard legislators one by one made statements. Most of them wanted to reduce government spending and most talked about cutting programs that the poor and people on welfare depend on—things like the utility subsidy and school lunch programs."

Kevin then picked up the narrative.

"Yeah, they barely gave us ten minutes to speak and when our people got up to the microphone a number of the legislators got up and walked out for a smoke, or to get a Coke. Those who stayed weren't paying any attention at all. Some started writing while others turned to the person next to them and started talking. They were just plain rude. But Sr. Grace gave 'em hell."

The room briefly erupted in approval and Grace raised her fist and smiled modestly in appreciation. Kevin continued, now laughing as he recalled the scene,

"She got up to the microphone and started yelling at those suits calling them all phonies and hypocrites. She went on and on about how they lined their own pockets with money they stole from the poor. You can be sure they paid attention when she started callin' 'em by name and givin' everyone an earful about the posh lives this or that legislator lived and how some were living off family money or spent their lives barely succeeding in family owned businesses that had been handed to them by their parents."

"You had em' goin' Gracie," said Tricky Dick, offering his concise summary of Kevin's tale. Grace responded in her best impersonation of a World Wrestling Federation taunt:

"And I'll do it again. You just let me at 'um'"

Greg wrapped up the evening's description by presenting his version of the denouement:

"Security dragged her off the microphone after about five minutes and it looked like they were going to arrest her, but I think they realized at the last moment what a public relations fiasco that would be, so they just escorted her outside."

After a brief pause I offered my reflections.

"Sounds pretty exciting to me. It didn't sound altogether unsuccessful. You had a chance to speak and you even disrupted the flow of the meeting," I said, thinking that maybe they just had not seen the positive side of the picture.

"Yes," said Grace, "but the next day when the event was reported in the media, none of our comments made the news. Everything the legislature said became part of the public record; while everything we said simply was summed up under the heading, 'protest.' It was business as usual, and, 'oh yeah, a bunch of cranks from the Mercy House showed up and made a stink.' They even got our name wrong. How anonymous and voiceless can you get?! This time we want to get our message across loud and clear!"

Mortified that I never read the local section of the paper, where this story appeared, and because I was, more than likely, watching the Simpsons the evening that the story aired, I stammered into my response to Grace:

"Uh…well…uh…have you had any ideas during the last month about how you might go about getting your message across differently at this next meeting?" I queried in a weak attempt to recover from my attack of embarrassment and guilt. Grace slammed the ball back into my court.

"Well, we did discuss a few things, but we were hoping you would have some suggestions."

I was hoping the same thing, but my suggestion slate was completely blank, so instead I took a different approach.

"Maybe we need to first get clear about what it is we believe concerning these issues, then we might know better what it is we want to say, and how we ought to go about saying it?"

Spontaneous affirmations around the table encouraged me to proceed.

"Some of this stuff we have already gone over previously, but I think it deserves repeating in this context so we can get a better grasp of our message and our mission. Systems of oppression are, by their nature, dehumanizing. In this instance, the oppressive system has identified a target for dehumanization—the so-called 'welfare queen.' Onto the 'welfare queen' are projected all kinds of unflattering characteristics which have the cumulative effect of stripping away any shred of dignity that might have existed. Meanwhile, all welfare recipients become potential targets of this sort of slander. Therefore, anyone who is poor or receives a welfare check in this hostile climate is dehumanized because they have had their dignity robbed from them through repetition of the mantra: 'welfare queen.'"

I paused to check this out with the forum.

"Sounds right to me." Prince mumbled into his hand.

"So how do we stop them from oppressing us?" Asked Greg. I continued.

"You see, this is where I think we often go wrong. We think of oppression as the isolated actions of a few people against a larger group of hapless victims. I believe oppression is better understood as a system in which we all play a role, even if that role is unconsciously performed. For instance, it is important to realize that the oppressor class is not denying its oppression because it is being consciously deceptive. For the most part, they honestly don't perceive their role in society as oppressive. In a similar way, the oppressed also usually deny their oppression. As most twelve-step programs have taught us, people will stubbornly remain in denial until they are forced by circumstances to face the lie they have been living. Twelve step programs aptly name this 'hitting rock bottom.'"

I paused to see if I was loosing anyone. It was C.W.'s turn to ask for clarification:

"So how does viewing oppression as a system rather than as the actions of a few individuals against the rest of us make a difference for us in our situation?"

I proceeded.

"Well, it makes a big difference in how we approach our task. If dehumanization is a foundation of the current system of domination and not simply the random act of individuals, then liberation must be aimed against that system and not primarily at those individuals who are in positions of power in that system. In this way, liberation is not an act of reversing the roles of oppressor and oppressed, as tempting as that image might be. A reversal of roles changes nothing. An oppressive system would still reign supreme. Is everyone with me on this?"

Thoughtful nods encouraged me onwards.

"When we truly understand the systemic nature of oppression, our task becomes clearer as we realize we must liberate both the oppressed and the oppressor from a system that is mutually dehumanizing."

Suddenly Grace's face lit up and she sat erect in her chair with her hands palms down on the table as she gave voice to her epiphany:

"That way, when we fight against the dehumanized image of the 'welfare queen' we aren't just confronting the legislators with the humanity of the poor. We are making them face their own true humanity—their *Imago Dei*. It's good news for them and us, even though it may not be experienced that way."

Echoing Grace's revelation, I concluded my thoughts.

"Exactly. When the full humanity of one group in society is diminished, that has unforeseen repercussions for our definition of humanity as a whole. Membership in full humanity becomes reduced to an arbitrary set of characteristics or achievements. In contemporary North American society, full humanity is jeopardized by racism, sexism and classism. As Grace pointed out, we have a divine mandate to resist these dehumanizing forces and to reaffirm the full and complete humanity of everyone."

The next few hours were spent clarifying the concepts of systemic oppression and dehumanization. I volunteered to stand at the green-board that was propped up against a wall resting on a donated sofa table and record the conversation. One had to hold onto the board while writing with tiny chalk pieces that were flimsy and frequently popped out from between the two fingers holding them. Fruit-of-the-Loom underwear stuffed in a box under the sofa table ended up as my erasure. It occurred to me only after numerous erasures of the board that I had not checked the freshness of my tool. My role at the green-board was to play both auctioneer and court reporter as ideas and concepts arose, were discussed, and finally adopted by the forum or discarded. Only half of the group could spell well enough to play this role effectively and I had already had my say as forum catalyst; therefore, the role of official forum recorder fell logically to me.

In the course of our dialogue it was clear that, not only did we need to understand these ideas of systemic oppression and dehumanization, we wanted to find a way to convey them to the outside world. Simply stepping up to a microphone and delivering a prepared statement had not proven itself to be the most effective means of communication. We could be effectively tuned out, ignored, or marginalized using this method. The forum agreed that it would be necessary to get our point across in such a way that it would attract extended media coverage, which would not be mere sound bites designed to tell the public *that* we had protested, but rather a kind of coverage with enough information to tell the public *why* we were protesting.

We also wanted our protest to convey our religious convictions concerning this issue of dehumanization. Our identity as Catholic Christians needed to stand out so that we could be witnesses for a God of justice, love, mercy, forgiveness and truth. It was our intention to convey a message stressing these religious convictions, while maintaining a kind of universality so that it could be heard and embraced by those who did not share our perspective.

The weather on the day of the County Legislator's Meeting had been cool and overcast. It was late May, but it felt more like early November. I left work and hurried home to snatch a couple of bites to eat. I was noticeably anxious, more so than usual for a County Legislator's meeting. This feeling seemed out of place since my role that evening would be to sing second tenor in a choir of very modest talent. Maybe I had performance anxiety, I thought, but that just didn't seem to ring true. In my mind I went over our plan for the evening step-by-step, and discovered the source of my angst in the poster we had created and the powerful symbols associate with that sign, still eager and fresh from their success with the stop sign incident. Greg and Kevin had naturally assumed the leadership role for our protest that evening at the County Courthouse. The Forum had decided to stage a street drama that would include a black mother and her son standing under a poster, which read:

> She is a teenager
> She is poor
> She is homeless
> She is pregnant
> She is unmarried
> The identity of the father of her child is uncertain
> Is She
> Mary the Mother of Jesus?
> Or
> A Welfare Queen?

The rest of us were to form a choir off to the side, singing black spiritual renditions of the Ave Maria and other traditional Catholic hymns dedicated to the Mother of Jesus. Flyers would be handed out to passersby, which delivered the same message as the poster.

After finding a parking space in the relatively unfamiliar territory of downtown Rochester, I found my way to the Courthouse navigating by instinct. Due to time constraints, I had decided to come on my own rather than join the group in the House of Mercy van. The rest of the Forum had been there a few minutes by the time I showed up on the scene and Greg was nervously giving stage directions to our Madonna, while Kevin rehearsed with the choir. After exchanging familiar hugs and greetings with C.W., Rita and Gloria, I stepped to the side in order to better observe the odd collective behavior of the Forum as it unfolded on Rochester's Main St. that evening. At one and the same time no one and everyone was "in charge" of this event. Although Greg and Kevin were unofficially "in charge," they had delegated sufficient authority to lay the groundwork for the general chaos I was witnessing. In my experience, anarchy is highly participatory, yet only marginally efficient. Eventually our show would come together, but 6:00pm was approaching fast and a few legislators had already arrived.

Just then, Grace burst through the doors of the Courthouse and swooped over to C.W., Rita and Gloria. I could see by the urgent look on her face that something interesting was about to transpire so I nuzzled my way back into the circle just in time to hear Grace's announcement:

"We need to get moving. Some of the legislators have already gone in." She paused looking away from us to a distant, but approaching object. She pointed and declared:

"Look the television reporters are pulling up in their van."

Turning to the entire group she continued speaking, clapping her hands as she said,

"Come on people, let's go! The cameras are here. Look sharp!"

Grace's words always carried a degree of authority that no one else's enjoyed—not even C.W.'s or Rita's. The ragtag, anarchist gathering, fumbling around in front of the Courthouse, suddenly sobered up and snapped to attention, all of us taking our appropriate positions and assuming our various roles. I took my place in the choir wedging myself between Prince and Mrs. Washington, as the television cameras set up and the reporters did some preparatory interviews.

The House of Mercy had been contacted by two of the local television stations and the local newspaper about a week before to see if we were planning to protest this County Legislator's meeting like we had the previous month. For now, at least, we were an interesting commodity for a bored and depoliticized public. However, being a commodity meant being both used and abused by the media. Never a subject and always an object in relation to media interest, our public image would vacillate dramatically between good servants of the poor, crazy people in need of an avocation, and angry fanatics looking for a night in jail. Public curiosity and the media's satisfaction of that curiosity could cut both ways…as it did that night.

As we started to sing the first song in our small repertoire, a crowd of people gathered around consisting of legislators, media personnel, courthouse employees and passersby. As we completed the first verse of Ave Maria a woman's voice could be heard shouting an expletive followed by the figure of that same woman storming into the courthouse building. The crowd quickly polarized between those who supported us and those who considered our little street drama a disgraceful blasphemy. Some tried to shout us down, pointing fingers in our faces, while invoking epithets accusing us of impiety, disloyalty and shameful exhibitionism. Others defended us by shouting back at the individuals who were defaming our action—some of the confrontations even coming close to physical violence.

Although we kept singing, and our poster remained attached to the wall of the Courthouse, and our Madonna kept standing there defiantly with her child in her arms, the real story was clearly the melee that we had unwittingly catalyzed. Television cameras turned away from us, and reporters began interviewing the bystanders—both pro and con. On the evening news and in the paper the next morning we were "that group from the 'Mercy House' that had caused a disturbance in front of the Courthouse." Sound bite interviews with bystanders were interspersed with snapshot scenes of our street drama followed by extended commentary from the reporters. The distortion of our purpose that evening by the media was complete. Some of us would learn a hard lesson that night. Some of us would learn the wrong one.

During our ten-minute 'disturbance' most of us were transfixed by the spontaneous mob debate that our little street drama had spawned. However, intermittently my attention was drawn to Greg who was having a completely unique reaction to the rancor and vitriol of half of our audience. At first worried, his expression gradually became sad and despondent as he physically shrank back away from the crowd behind his fellow choir members. Both author and performer, each hateful barb of his critics struck Greg with the efficiency and accuracy of a cruise missile. In the end, a talented, intelligent, articulate, energetic, though emotionally defenseless, prophet leaned hunched over against the Courthouse wall with his head hung low examining his feet as they kicked lifelessly at the cracks in the pavement. While the rest of us laughed the incident off nervously retelling the hysteria we all had just endured, it was apparent that Greg was laughing bitterly and ironically at his own decisive defeat.

That night I picked up the Bible to read a chapter from one of the gospels as I always did before going to bed. As fortune would have it, I had reached chapter six of the Gospel of Luke, which included Luke's version of the Beatitudes. I thought to myself that reading the Beatitudes would be comforting after a day like this. Instead, the words were hard and the message was bracing like a sudden, unexpected slap in the face.

> Blessed are you when people hate you,
> and when they exclude and insult you
> and denounce your name as evil
> on account of the Son of Man.
> Rejoice and leap for joy on that day!
> behold your reward
> will be great in heaven. For their
> ancestors treated the prophets
> in the same way.

Greg had all the ingredients of a great leader and a legendary prophet, save one—an armor-plated exoskeleton. The harsh prophetic stage would always be foreign territory for someone as sensitive as

Greg. Although Greg continued to work with the Forum, something intangible, though essential, was lost in the pummeling his spirit took that evening.

Swords into Plowshares

On nice days I rode my bike to work at the House of Mercy, and today was shaping up to be one of those nearly perfect summer days. The touring bike I rode was poorly maintained. Only a few of the gears worked some of the time and the front brake dragged with a rhythmic regularity on the rim. In addition to the marginal condition of the bike was the fact that I always wore a half-filled canvas backpack which awkwardly rolled left and right around my back. My average bike ride to work was something of an Oregon-Trail adventure, even if one didn't factor in the traffic and deteriorating road conditions. As I purposefully rode that crisp and clear morning I passed through several strange warm and humid patches in the air. It felt like the air temperature rose and fell ten degrees as I passed in and out of these atmospheric pockets. I wondered if these were a foretaste of things to come that day—episodes of heated discomfort punctuating an otherwise uneventful chain of events.

The conditions of the roads deteriorated as I rode from downtown into the slums of the northern neighborhoods; however, these days the roads were especially primitive due to the construction work that had begun in preparation for the new middle school at the corner of Scio Street and Central Park Avenue—across the street from the House of Mercy. On the way, smooth pavement turned into rough concrete which quickly gave way to dirt and gravel. Persistent truck and automobile traffic maintained a cloud of dirt which hung in the humid air over

Scio Street. The harder one worked to navigate a hostile terrain on bike, the heavier one breathed, and the heavier one breathed, the more road dirt one swallowed. By the time I would reach the House of Mercy each morning it all seemed like a nefarious plot against my best intentions to save the earth from the automobile—at least from my automobile.

Demolition of the neighborhood had already started and the current building used by the House of Mercy was slated to be razed before the end of the summer. The dirty, desolate, destroyed and demolished landscape that spread a full half square mile to the south and west of the House of Mercy was reminiscent of scenes from Beruit and other urban war zones. Most pathetic of all were the skeletal remains of half-demolished buildings left overnight by construction crews eager to clock out for the evening. These teetering shells were a hazard for neighborhood children who could not resist the allure of these unwrapped gifts of adventure.

On this particular morning, one of the shells in particular had drawn a group of a half dozen gradeschool-aged boys. Their game was some version of cops and robbers, or possibly the reenactment of a war, with stick guns and brick grenades. As they played, one could witness glee mixed with anger, mixed with sadness and then mirth, all very fleeting and none of it very serious. Occasionally, a momentary impasse would halt the action as rules were invented, broken, enforced or rewritten to better fit the mood of the game. The point was to have fun, but the spirit of the game could be deadly serious. I wondered how many of these same boys would be packing and using the real thing in a matter of a few years. The nostalgic recollections of my own childhood days spent playing strikingly similar games under almost identical circumstances mingled with the present scenario in such a paradoxical way that I had to wonder what exactly differentiated the apparent innocence of the one from the obvious gravity of the other. The only answer which made sense was that, at one point or another, my peers and I had been disarmed.

Without fully coming to a stop I slipped my feet out of the toe clips and dismounted, immediately picking up the bike in a single motion of unbroken momentum. My daily rehearsal of this dismount had made it second nature and it expended less energy than the usual stop-and-go dismount. I deposited my bike in the hallway and headed for Sr. Grace's office, but before I had taken more than a few steps, C.W. spied me from the kitchen.

"Hey Tom!" How yah doin'?" He asked

"Fine." I shot back.

"Grace asked me to ask you if you wouldn't mind working with me today with the food distribution. We're expecting about twice the normal load this month." C.W. said this as he stuffed a loaf of bread in a bag he had been carefully packing. As he placed the bag on the floor next to the countless others he and some volunteers had already packed, I responded.

"Sure, that sounds great. What do you want me to do?"

"Bag groceries. It's as simple as that," C.W. said as he extended his hand holding the first of what would become innumerable grocery bags needing to be stuffed that morning. I started haphazardly bagging under the watchful and experienced eyes of C.W. After a few attempts he began offering pointers.

"Place the heavier and more durable stuff at the bottom, like the potatoes, canned food, and the milk. Put the softer, lighter and perishable things on top… Be sure to place a few sugary goodies in for the kids."

Before long I had the hang of it and I was getting into a groove along with the rest of the volunteers. When basic instruction was no longer an issue, C.W. turned to more serious topics.

"You know, everybody appreciates the fact that you ride your bike here every morning."

I was surprised by C.W.'s comment. It hadn't occurred to me that anyone was paying any attention to me whatsoever, let alone that some were so attuned to my behavior that they were receiving the environmental message attached to my daily bike ride. I was both flattered and encouraged as I responded to C.W.'s announcement.

"Really?! I didn't know there were that many people around who were concerned about the environment. Maybe we should take that up as an issue in the Forum."

C.W. paused like a cat listening for the faint sound of prey amidst the cacophony of background noise. A puzzled look on his face resolved and his workflow resumed as he continued the conversation.

"Uh, no, that's not what I meant. Everyone appreciates your bike riding because that means you get around like the rest of us who, for the most part, use our feet or our bikes. As you know, many people here are too poor to own a car. You have chosen the poor person's method of getting from one place to another and you seem to prefer it. You get off your bike every day and talk about how wonderful it is to get exercise and breath fresh air—how much better it is than driving a car. You may not see it, but that little ride and those short comments really raise the morale around here. It makes us feel superior to those who own cars.

Even though most here don't choose to walk and bike to wherever we go, it seems now that we do choose not to drive and that we have chosen the better part."

I wasn't expecting to hear that, and now it was my turn to pause like a cat caught with its paw in the fishbowl and give C.W. a momentary puzzled look. Articulately I responded.

"Uh...wow...I had no idea..." C.W. saved me from what would have been a disastrously superficial comment by interrupting my nascent train of thought with a practical concern.

"Yah know, you really should lock your bike. I have a hard time keeping my eye on it all day, being I'm in and out, here and there, doing all kinds of things."

"I'm sorry, you're right. Grace mentioned that to me last week, but I just forgot to go buy a lock. I'll get one today if I get a break in the afternoon." I replied.

"People around here are generally good, but they're also dirt poor. It's just not fair to throw too many temptations—like a free bike—in their path day after day. Yah know, it's not just guys like Forrest who will steal a nice bike like yours." C.W. wisely counseled me as fresh images of Forrest Hope filled my conscious thoughts.

Forrest appeared on the scene only a few days after I had arrived, just having been released from prison for armed robbery. He was the friend of a friend who had been a guest at the House of Mercy a few years back. Forrest had expressed to his friend, in no uncertain terms, that he wanted to turn his life around for the better, now that he had learned his lesson behind bars. And so he showed up at our door ready and willing to receive whatever miraculous fix we had to offer for his broken and tattered life.

None of the staff had ever met Forrest before, which kind of made me feel a special bond for him. From the moment I had arrived a few days before, I had been working feverishly to get to know the names and personalities of the various guests whom everyone else, of course, already knew. Forrest was a great equalizer for me. I would get to know him at the same time everyone else did, and there was a peculiar satisfaction in that experience.

Forrest made a very positive first impression on everyone. He dressed in a white shirt and a black tie, with dress slacks and patent leather shoes that were a size or two on the large side. He stood a little shy of six feet and he had a powerful, muscular frame that was accentuated, in an odd way, by his ill-fitting attire. He was an African

American around the age of twenty-eight who had a light complexion and he wore his hair closely cropped. A scar that ran down the side of his right cheek would disappear on days when he would forget to shave. If you were speaking with Forrest you would find yourself locked in his intense gaze for the duration of the conversation. If you moved, his eyes would follow. Though he might be pondering a question, his eyes would never release you from captivity. If you looked away in distraction or abstraction, he was sure to step into your line of sight if he could. Forrest's very presence made an impression that was, at one and the same time, both acute and unsettling.

In his first few days at the House of Mercy, Forrest was almost painfully polite, addressing everyone by a title, correctly or incorrectly applied. No one at the House of Mercy had ever used my academic title, but as soon as Forrest heard I was a "doctor" he would not address me otherwise. Of course, one of the reasons I didn't want people to apply the title was because I was certain I would then be confused for someone in the medical profession. Sure enough, Forrest and a number of other guests began coming to me for consultation on their medical conditions. When I demurred and offered an explanation of the term "doctor," Forrest interrupted explaining that he would be happy to pay for my services as soon as he had a job. I spent weeks deconstructing the expectations of a house-load of guests who had overheard one or more of Forrest's exchanges with me.

Forrest was also enthusiastic. He spent his first few days following C.W. around and performing small chores at his command. When he had exhausted C.W.'s surplus needs he would sit in my office and ask questions about the sorts of things I did. Since I was still trying to figure that out for myself, these conversations were sometimes a little contrived, though they did force me to think at a very early stage about what role I thought I should play there. Forrest was, after only a few weeks, becoming a fixture in our little home. Although he was high maintenance on an interpersonal level, he was very polite, eager to please and could even be sporadically helpful to C.W. It was beginning to look like we had successfully adopted another orphan off the streets who was showing real signs of becoming a productive, contributing member of the community.

And then, one day, Forrest just stopped coming. At first, no one gave it a second thought, but then, when the staff began asking around, the answer they received was alarming. Forrest had met up with some old buddies who were selling crack cocaine and he just couldn't resist the allure of that demanding mistress. Reports from the street confirmed Forrest's seduction. He spent his time between indulging his crack habit, picking fights with friends and strangers alike, and begging money from acquaintances to satisfy his rekindled addiction. The main fear was that it would only be a matter of time before Forrest would hurt someone or get caught with his hands in the cookie jar. Even those who knew him best were not immune from fearing him and even avoiding him because he had that "wild look" in his eyes. While I reserved judgment for the moment, it wouldn't be long before we could all see for ourselves what a crackhead extraordinaire Forrest had become in a virtual overnight metamorphosis. In this case, the butterfly had returned to the cocoon only to reemerge in an uglier and definitively more primitive state.

The next time I saw Forrest he was dressed head to toe in army fatigues, complete with a camouflage hat and a pair of black leather boots. He was pacing the hallways of the House of Mercy hoping to find a fresh victim to massage his maniacal ego. I was coming in the front door and was surprised to find the place practically empty. When our eyes met across the empty hallway I could see his expression change from that of a caged lion to that of a predator with its prey in sight. As I came up the short flight of stairs he strode towards me with a hurried and purposeful stride. We met at the top of the stairs.

"You think you can take me don't you?" He challenged, poking his finger in my chest. I had worked with manipulative personalities for more than a decade while working with the disabled so I immediately put my skills to good use. Without skipping a beat I cheerfully and casually greeted him.

"Hi, Forrest, I haven't seen you in a couple of weeks. What's happening?"

"You wanna' know what's happening man? They're ignoring me! That's what's happening! Look, they shut the door in my face and locked it behind them! They fuckin' chicken! You hear me C.W.?! Chicken!" he said, all of this while gesturing wildly at the door to Grace's office. I glanced in that direction and, sure enough, it was closed, which also indicated it was locked given the lack of a knob and latch. That was not a good sign, and for the first time I felt frightened. Had I just walked into something that was going to turn really ugly? My office was on the second floor so I started to move in that direction as I responded to Forrest's agitated comments:

"Well don't take it personally. They're very busy people and probably just needed to make some phone calls."

Forrest jumped in my path before I could take more than a few steps. He was escalating his concocted conflict.

"You think you can kick my ass don't you?!"

"Forrest, I'm sure you could beat me up, no problem whatsoever. It's not even worth testing that theory." I said, maintaining a casual and friendly demeanor.

"You got that right, cause I'm a bad motha' fucker! B...A...D... bad, motha fucker!" Forrest barked furiously. I tried to redirect his attention to practical tasks.

"Do you know where C.W. is? I need to talk to him about something?" I said, hoping to switch Forrest out of his anger and into a problem-solving mode. But he couldn't be sidetracked.

"You think you're pretty fast don't you?" I heard you ran track in college. Well, I'll tell you what. I challenge you right here and now to a race—right out there on the streets—me in my boots and you in your running shoes. Whaddaya say?" I wondered where the hell I had let that little tidbit from my past slip out in conversation. The things that can come back to haunt you when dealing with borderline personalities are truly amazing. I tried to stroke his ego once again to see if he could be satisfied that way.

"Forrest, I'm sure you can win any footrace you run against me. I think it would just be a waist of your energy proving to everyone what we already know: you are the fastest."

"You jus' chicken! You a fuckin' chicken bastard like those fuckers in there! Those dirty motha' fuckers behind that door!" Forrest was no longer addressing me, but was shouting and gesticulating at Sr. Grace's office door. He was sweating profusely now and the veins on his neck stood out. I was running our of items in my bag of tricks and Forrest seemed no closer to letting me off the hook than when he began. Suddenly the muffled voice of C.W. emerged from behind the closed door.

"Don't make me come out there Forrest."

"Or what! Or fuck..." The office door abruptly swung open and C.W.'s imposing figure strode out interrupting Forrest's rage.

"You need to leave, now." C.W. commanded, pointing to the door.

"Or what? What you..." Forrest did not get to finish before C.W. trumped him with his resounding baritone.

"I have many options, Forrest. I have options you can't even imagine. And I am ready to exercise those options right now." C.W. said, again pointing to the door. Forrest paused and stared at the confident, heroic, statuesque figure of C.W., apparently summing up the situation and then slowly backed away toward the side door tossing extemporaneous threats at C.W. and the rest of the House of Mercy personnel. C.W. stoically held Forrest in his gaze until he had disappeared from view. He then leaned towards Grace's office turning his head to announce:

"The coast is clear."

A cheer rose from the group assembled in Grace's office. C.W. and I then joined the others in Grace's office for a debriefing on Forrest's behavior that day. He had already been in a fight with Tracy on the street in front of the House of Mercy. Tracy was a young African American man around Forrest's age who was diagnosed with a type of schizophrenia. He was generally harmless and at times even humorous, but he bummed cigarettes, money and other things from anyone and everyone, so he wasn't the most popular person either. Tracy tried to bum cigarettes from Forrest and the response was a slug in the face. He held his own for a while, but ultimately his wiry frame was no match for the muscle and mass that Forrest possessed.

Rita had spent the morning tending to Tracy's bruised body and ego. Eventually Forrest brought his reign of terror inside the House of Mercy, which effectively cleared the place out in record time. He made such a nuisance of himself that Grace became exasperated and locked her door. One by one, other staff made their way to Grace's office as Forrest broke them down—testing, taunting and tormenting them with his pointless aggression. Finally, the whole staff was in Grace's office save me. That's when I came through the front door.

Forrest never returned that day. By the afternoon of the following day the word on the street said that Forrest had been arrested the night before while breaking into someone's home. He had been on probation so he was sure to go back to prison for an offence like that. The word on the street was usually pretty accurate and this instance would prove to be no exception to the rule. We wouldn't be seeing Forrest for at least a year and no one seemed too awfully broken up at the thought of having an extended vacation away from him.

My recollections of our recent experiences with Forrest were interrupted when C.W. took me aside to explain the developing situation in our food distribution project. He had been in the back room for some time reading, calculating and counting heads as the rest of us continued to stuff groceries into bags. He was wearing his reading glasses which gave him a more officious presence and accentuated his facial expressions. He was clearly concerned, but his glasses heightened his expression of urgency which made me all the more attentive as he explained our supply side dilemma.

"It looks like we are going to run out of food before we run out of people." Naively, I retorted,

"Would you like me to go out and tell the people at the end of the line that there might not be enough food?" C.W.'s eyes bulged with shock and he stretched his hands out towards me in a halting motion.

"God no! We'll have a riot or a war on our hands if we do that! We'll wait until we get down to our last few bags before we try to soften the blow. Otherwise, the strong will start to take advantage of the weak as they jockey for position in line."

"Well, why are you telling me and not the other staff and volunteers." I asked wondering why C.W. had called this semi-confidential conference.

"Because they get what's left over and today there are going to be few real rewards for being a House of Mercy volunteer." C.W. said with a shrug of his shoulders and his eyebrows raised in an exaggerated way like the kids on the Little Rascals. C.W. looked around again checking for eavesdroppers and then continued,

"I'm going to allow each of them to set aside one bag of groceries in the store room for themselves and then have you supervise them as they bring the bags of food from the kitchen to the back room, as we pass bags out the window. When all the bags are out of the kitchen, tell them to get their groceries and exit through the front door where they probably can avoid being spotted by people in line."

"What will happen when we have no more food?" I asked, not really sure I wanted to hear. C.W. obliged:

"Don't ask… It's usually not pretty."

It wasn't a comforting reply, but my one consolation was that C.W. was anything but a bullshitter. A straight answer was what I had sought and that is precisely what I got. I assembled the troops and laid out the plan of attack. Our volunteers were veterans of these scarcity induced battles so experience had prepared them well to execute this little ruse of ours without a hitch.

And so the assembly line was set in motion as C.W. opened the back window and took the benefits card from the first person standing in line. He would quickly scan the dates, names and photograph on the card and then write down pertinent pieces of information on a legal pad before returning the card to the owner. On C.W.'s command, I would then hand out a bag of groceries, while the next person began the clerical process with C.W. After about twenty people we had achieved maximum efficiency and we were distributing about one hundred and fifty bags per hour. We had packed over two hundred and fifty bags and when there were about fifty left, our volunteers ducked into the cooler, grabbed their bags, and slipped unruffled out the front door. C.W. and I were not so lucky.

My attention kept shifting nervously from C.W., to the line of people that stretched around the side of the building, to the person receiving the groceries I was handing out. As I handed groceries down, I wanted to tell people to get while the getting was good, but that, of course, would have let the cat out of the bag, so to say. I searched C.W.'s face for signs of panic or even mild worry, but he never let on that we were rapidly coming to the end of our resources. He was a masterful bluffer and I was glad neither of us had a penchant for poker because I couldn't bluff my way through a preschool game of Go Fish. I also vainly hoped that the end of the line would appear around the corner after each successive recipient left with his or her booty. When there were about ten bags left, C.W. took a long look at the remaining bags, then an equally long look at the remaining queue, and finally he gazed at me over his reading glasses and said in an ominous tone:

"It's time."

With that C.W. put down the legal pad and stuck his head out the window, still enthroned in the wooden chair as he had been throughout the process.

"We have only ten bags left..." Before he could complete the announcement shouts, boos and moans from the crowd drowned him out. C.W. began again.

"We have only ten bags left. The next ten people in line will receive food. Now I know these people, so don't try to cheat or jump in front of anyone. For the rest of you, we are very sorry, but we have distributed all of the food we received." A man's voice bitterly retorted:

"Yeah, 'cept for all that food you give to yo favorites."

"Yeah, where them pet volunteers a yours?" Cried a woman's voice.

As more disgruntled and impolite comments wafted into the room, I could see through the side window the news spread gradually to the back of the line. Most people mumbled something and walked away with their head hung in disappointment. Others shouted obscenities in our direction and punched the air in fury. A few kicked or slapped the building as they walked down the driveway to go back home. Suddenly, a baseball-sized rock flew through the open window barely missing C.W.'s head. It struck the wood door jam knocking out a sizeable chip on its way to rest on the floor. I immediately backed up against an adjacent wall in order to become a more difficult target. C.W., who had been writing down information from a benefits card, placed his legal pad to the side and once again calmly stuck his head out the window. I was horrified and almost lunged for him to preserve him from any of the other budding Dwight Goodings lurking in the back yard. But C.W. fearlessly started scolding the riff raff.

"Those who are not receiving food please get the hell out of here. The person who threw the rock does not want to force me to come out there and return the favor. Now…MOVE IT!"

C.W. drew his head back in and continued processing the remaining recipients. After a moment of silence he offered these words of wisdom, with a smirk sneaking through under his reading glasses:

"In some ways you've gotta believe you are unafraid so you can make them believe the same…Even if you are scared shitless."

When all of the food was gone and the crowds had all dispersed, C.W. and I retired to Grace's office to take a well-deserved break. Grace, of course, was there with someone who needed an advocate to plead her case at the Department of Social Services. Greg and Kevin were also in the room and their attention was so fully taken by events in the lot outside Grace's window that they did not even acknowledge us when we greeted them by name. They were laughing, gesturing and poking each other as they sustained a running commentary on events that remained out of sight for most of the rest of the room's inhabitants.

"Soup Bone jes' won't let her be!" Greg said, delighted by the spectacle, but sobered by previous experiences with this particular conflict.

"He better back down before Toni wops him upside his drunk-ass head." Kevin replied, big eyed and looking around the room, finally realizing that he and Greg had an audience. Kevin nudged Greg who turned to find most of the room fixed on their play-by-play account. After a brief wave and nod of their heads, Kevin and Greg returned to the drama unfolding outside Grace's window.

"Where's she goin'?" Kevin asked with a puzzled expression mixed with a hint of disappointment that their source of afternoon entertainment had suddenly abandoned them. Greg leaned forward in his chair to follow Toni's apparent retreat.

"Looks like she's headin' home…an' Soup Bone's makin' like he's the king of Shit Mountain."

Both he and Kevin laughed as most of the rest of us began huddling around the window to share vicariously in Soup Bone's winner-circle celebration with a group of well-wishers who had gathered in the lot to cheer one or the other on. Toni and Soup Bone always provided a bizarre spectacle that combined passionate devotion with violent outburst of rancor. Toni Walker was a solid African American woman who stood just shy of six feet tall and resembled a football player from behind. She walked, talked, cussed and fought like a man, and she struck a formidable pose when someone would challenge her position. Her demeanor was mercurial and her days seemed to be spent swept this way and that by extreme and conflicting emotional states that were partly her nature and partly nurtured by various combinations of street medicinals. The House of Mercy staff was always on the lookout toward the advent of a new month because that was when social service checks arrived and, in turn, the medicinals would flow. Toni, Soup Bone and many other regular guests were known to make life miserably interesting around this time of the month—at least until the money ran out.

By contrast, Toni's common-law spouse was descriptively named. McClendon Robinson's small and scrawny body brought to mind a variety of less than flattering symbols, but the one that ultimately stuck was Soup Bone. He was a singularly unintimidating man, affable and energetic, with just a hint of mischief behind darting eyes and a semi-permanent smirk. Even fully medicated, Soup Bone was generally easy to be around. He was a "happy drunk" for everyone save one—Toni Walker—who tragically had so many buttons that could be so easily pushed. The devil in Soup Bone struggled to contain himself even when the drug and alcohol well had run dry. However, when the spirits were flowing freely, he gloried in the mission of taunting Toni into a frenzy over one frivolity or another. He toyed with her like a puppet master until all hell would break loose on himself and a whole host of other victims who ran the gamut from collusive conspirators to innocent bystanders. In this instance, Kevin and Greg had played a role that placed them somewhere in the middle.

"Toni just walked away? I can't believe that. That's not like her at all." Grace said with a smile, taking a break from her counseling to contribute to an interpretation of a drama that had apparently come to an abrupt and unexpected denouement. Greg chimed in:

"Looks like she's lettin' Soup Bone have this round."

"Yeah, I think she's gone home for good." Kevin added.

Those of us now gathered around the window continued to mirthfully report the details of Soup Bone's premature celebration as he gave high-fives to friends and yelled obscenities in the direction of Toni's departure, pointing authoritatively with his hand over his head. Toni had indeed gone home, but it wouldn't be for good. Those of us purveying the revelry of Soup Bone and his friends in the vacant lot had all but forgotten Toni, whom we now believed had given up the fight. She had exited stage left and the celebration was gradually milling its way to our right, returning victoriously to the House of Mercy. We spectators were busy summarizing the event and offering our expert opinions on the various issues raised by the conflict, as well as the unexpected restraint of Toni. Kevin was the first to notice our conclusions were premature.

"Uh-oh, here she comes back for round two." He said pointing out the window at Toni's advancing figure. With a furious expression and an aggressive stride, Toni pounded her way across the lot like a juggernaut—all the while fixing Soup Bone in her line of fire.

"What's that in her hand?" Gloria asked as she set down the case file she had been reviewing moments before.

"She's got a knife!" Cried Greg. Sure enough, in Toni's right hand flashed a long kitchen knife that beamed like a lighthouse in the sunshine with each stride. She was advancing quickly on Soup Bone and his pit crew, none of whom had yet taken notice of their changing fortunes. Those nearest the window in Grace's office began yelling and knocking on the window in a vain attempt to get Soup Bone's attention. Moments before, Grace had interrupted her counseling session and headed for the window to witness these developments for herself. When she caught a glimpse of the impending one-woman onslaught she immediately assessed the situation for C.W.

"C.W., this looks serious!"

"I'm on it." C.W. said as he pulled his hat off of his face, sat up and let out a long breath. Then, in a single sudden motion, he stood up and walked out the door. C.W. had been slouching in a chair off to the side with his hat over his face trying to rest and ignore the mounting drama outside Grace's window. He had already absorbed more than his share of grief and vitriol on this hot summer afternoon and he had been praying Toni and Soup Bone would not add to his misery. Nonetheless, the call from Grace for his intervention obviously came as no surprise as the war-torn soldier dutifully and wearily made his way to the front lines.

When Toni was about 30 feet away from those prematurely celebrating Soup Bone's apparent victory, one of the celebrants caught sight of her charging body and shouted out a warning as he ran for his life. Like a swarm of cockroaches, the assembly scattered and scurried abandoning a bewildered Soup Bone as he turned just in time to face his rampaging beloved, who was now brandishing the weapon she had procured from their home.

"Oh, I can't look at this!" Kevin said as he stood, turned and strode away from the window. The mood at the window was now tense and sober. The few comments being made were informative and serious. As Grace tried to pry the window open with my help, Toni took her first swipe across the chest of Soup Bone with her knife. Soup Bone jumped backward and swung both arms out to the side momentarily striking a crucified pose in mid air as Toni's knife sliced open his shirt and left a bleeding horizontal gash across his left pectoral. By the look on her face, it was clear Toni knew she had hit flesh, and while Soup Bone blustered, cried and scrambled in reverse, she paused and assessed the damage she had inflicted, both proud of her accomplished revenge and yet remorseful for the pain it caused her beloved. Toni recomposed her rage after realizing the wound was skin-deep and began yelling at a bleeding Soup Bone who was himself assessing the damage while contrarily attempting to both tongue-lash and calm Toni. She still wielded the knife menacingly; however, her lunges were now manifestly fraudulent. The knife had accomplished its task of imposing superficial injury and instilling persistent fear in a partner who had crossed the fine line in Toni's delicately balanced psyche.

By the time C.W. arrived on the scene Toni was already attempting to defend her knife-wielding actions to Soup Bone and the others assembled. Fortunately for C.W., disarming Toni on this occasion would not require much more than an extended hand and a few firm and loving comments. As Toni gave up her knife, Sr. Rita tended to Soup Bone's wounds. After a brief assessment she put him in her car and took him to the emergency room for a few stitches. From 100 feet away, those of us still at the window could see the bemused roll of C.W.'s eyes as he hugged and comforted the linebacker-sized woman now gushing emotionally in his arms. Grace had joined the scene just before Rita took Soup Bone to the hospital and now helped C.W. escort Toni to Grace's office. Those of us left in Grace's office quickly filed out to make room for the heroes and fallen warriors. We made our way to the front room and most began weaving the tale that would become the legend of the day Toni went after Soup Bone with a kitchen knife.

I chose to sit quietly, reflecting on the events of that waning day, and taking in the dysfunctional hominess of the now peaceful House of Mercy. Frank Hayes, an elderly African American man who was occasionally flamboyantly gay, had been close to the action out on the "vacant lot of honor." As he recounted his version of the events that had transpired, I was struck by the behavior of his peers, who never treated him differently because of his sexual orientation. The only time I saw Frank singled out for his gayness was when Frank was seeking that kind of attention, as, for instance, was the case every Halloween when he would show up in full drag. There were many gay and lesbian people who frequented the House of Mercy and their sexual orientation was treated as something profoundly inconsequential. In the other mostly white, middle-class settings I had frequented, gay and lesbian people were treated like freakish sideshow characters who either deserved to be persecuted, or preserved like some rare species. Never before in my experience had a community modeled such equanimity toward gays and lesbians, and this seemed to me to be the most liberating environment of all. Equanimity bred a disarming honesty and openness. Over time, this community had lost its will to isolate, judge and condemn people who strayed from the sexual norm.

That day I learned many very important lessons. We all carry weapons on the street, whether they be stones, knives and guns, or more subtle weapons of prejudice, hate and discrimination. All of us need to be disarmed because the streets can be a frightening, violent and dangerous place. They can also be a place of mercy.

Empty Tombs

I crouched in my donated office chair—permanently adjusted to its lowest setting—staring at my office door, lodged as it was in a half-open, half-closed position. I would have to suffer this particular source of frustration and bruises one more day since I had neglected once again to pack my hammer and large screwdriver, which would have given me the means to take the door off its hinges. No part of the House of Mercy was ever actually level and that applied to my door jam as much as it did the window frame that was stuck shut in the middle of this long steamy season. A fan in the hallway basted me with hot attic air as I sat there reminding myself that the new, air-conditioned House of Mercy would soon be ready for occupation. Recently, C.W. had been spending a good portion of his days at the new location on Hudson Avenue assisting the engineers and construction crew in the renovation of the new property. He would occasionally drop in on the suffering remnant here at Central Park and gleefully recount the progress: new doors, new windows, new kitchen, new garage doors, and, of course, the new central air-conditioning unit perched on the roof. On that unusually hot July morning I had sweet visions of a new, spacious, cool and ventilated office with a computer and a new phone sitting on top of a steel desk with drawers that opened when you pulled on their handles.

With a shake of my head I snapped out of my reverie, stood up, and yanked once again on the handle of the top drawer of my desk. This only caused my desk to lurch half a foot away from the wall, making my already confined space that much more claustrophobic. The room had the size, décor, and feel of a no-frills casket. It was also buried in a corner of the house where no one but mad men and Englishmen would venture during the summer months, making this choice little spot as lively as a graveyard on days like these. The loneliness and morbid silence were usually not an issue for me since my grant writing duties normally required some isolation from the hustle and bustle of the first floor. However, this morning would not be productive regardless of the number or intensity of external distractions. Downstairs they were making preparations for Sweet Thing's funeral and I just couldn't get my mind off of his death. So I gave up trying to retrieve a pen from my drawer and shoved my desk back up against the wall. All of the quaking and jarring caused a stack of forms to fall to the floor. As I stared at the mess I had just created I decided I would abandon my plans to get some work done and go downstairs as soon as I got things back in order. Interred beneath the last stack of spilled forms lay a brand new box of pens.

As I held the box of pens in my hand, oddly savoring the mix of emotions inspired by its ironic and unexpected revelation, I heard the footsteps of someone brave enough to endure the near suffocating heat on the attic stairway. The voice talking to itself told me it was Tracy, who was likely coming to me hoping to find a sympathetic ear for his issue-of-the-day. Everyone downstairs was busier than usual and Tracy's issue probably had not received a satisfactory amount of attention and respect from this preoccupied audience. Realizing that I was destined to achieve nothing that day, I readied myself to greet Tracy who appeared in my half-open doorway in his typical attire: jeans, tank top and a multi-colored wool skull cap. Tracy stood about five feet nine inches tall, though he frequently slouched his shoulders in such a way that made him seem shorter. He had very smooth and rather light toned skin that was almost exactly the color of chocolate milk. His given name was Tracy, but he often asked people to call him "Abdul" in honor of his so-called Islamic heritage. Tracy knew precious little about Islam and, as often as not, disregarded his Muslim name. In my experience I found that if I called him "Abdul" he often did not acknowledge that I was addressing him. For the sake of expediency I had abandoned the practice of referring to him by his chosen name.

He was holding a book in one hand and pointing at the page with the other. He had been mumbling non-stop all the way up the stairs, but as he emerged in my doorway he became more animated, recognizing he had someone's undivided attention.

"The black man has let the white man make a fool of him. The black man has obediently taken on the white man's religion, politics, economy and culture and look where that has gotten the black man. We are still slaves. We still live in squalor while doing the white man's dirty work." Tracy delivered his message doing his best to impersonate the preachy, sermonizing style of a Civil Rights leader from the 1960's. I could now see he was pointing at a copy of Manning Marable's *How Capitalism Underdeveloped Black America*, which I had been using as a resource book with the Forum because we had been trying to analyze the effects of racism on poverty in Rochester. Apparently Tracy had been following our progress from the wings and doing some of his own independent homework.

In spite of his schizophrenia, which often made his delivery sound clownish and ridiculous, Tracy was quite intelligent. His disease frequently got in the way of his capacity to express what was on his mind in a coherent, serious and respectable manner. Tracy needed someone to talk to this morning, and it probably had nothing to do with the book. However, Tracy had gone to the trouble of reading the book so he would have something to talk to us about.

While I was sure Tracy felt strongly about the analysis of the American economy he had read in Manning Marable's book, I also suspected that Tracy had more pressing personal issues he needed to talk about. He and Sweet Thing had a friendly, tolerant relationship. Sweet Thing didn't mind sitting for hours in the kitchen next to Tracy and listening politely to his sometimes-meaningless verbiage. Sweet Thing was often a calming presence for Tracy who apparently needed to vent in these long pointless monologues in order to find peace within. Sweet Thing had blessed us all with his quiet and comforting gift of presence. For Tracy, that gift surely must have been profound. I wasn't sure how we were going to bridge the gulf between social theory and Sweet Thing, but I was willing to give it a shot.

"Hi, Tracy. Hey, what a coincidence, I see you've been reading Manning Marable's book just like we are in the Forum. So what do you think about it?" I asked.

"The MAN is always on the lookout so he can tell when you at the lowest of low points." Tracy began, apparently offering his interpretation of Marable's work. "You don't know it. You think you doin' just fine. In fact, things have never been better. But what you don't know is you just took the final step into the white man's trap an' POW! emancipation turns into a new an' more lethal kind of slavery. But black folks is just as much to blame. We took the bait when the white man started selling his shiny wares to us. We turned our backs on our own black merchants to take a seat at the table with the MAN. But what we got wasn't a seat at the table. We got shoved under the table with the dogs. With the goddamn dogs!" Tracy continued, but I will neglect his full twenty-minute summary of Marable's thesis for the sake of brevity. Nevertheless, it was clear that Tracy had gotten the gist of this fairly complex reading of American economic history, albeit with his own bizarre interpretive flair. When he came up for air I jumped on the chance to direct the conversation towards Sweet Thing.

"So what's going on downstairs?" I asked rhetorically—knowing full well that the rest of the staff were preparing for Sweet Thing's funeral.

Tracy paused uncharacteristically. I looked up and as our eyes met I could see by the look on his face that my question had caught him completely off guard. His eyes darted to the floor as he attempted to fill the silence.

"Busy, busy, busy. Always too fuckin' busy. Rushing like crazy niggers from the end of a bullwhip. I don't know what they're doin'. They don't even know what they're doin'." He mumbled this in a more subdued voice than his usual pulpit-proclamation delivery. His body language was also less kinetic. Something had turned his rheostat down. I continued with this line of inquiry.

"I heard they were preparing for Sweet Thing's funeral." I said, and again Tracy allowed a long silence before he responded. When he spoke his voice had a natural, unaffected quality to it. I had never heard Tracy speak this way.

"Yes they are, but they won't let me help." It was my turn to pause in surprise and I measured my next words carefully.

"How do you want to help?" I asked sincerely.

"I want to speak." Tracy said, his head still hung low.

"What would you say?" I asked, expecting the usual homiletic onslaught. Instead Tracy paused again, raising his left hand up and around the back of his head, then up over the top and down across his face as he leaned his right shoulder against my door jam. Finally, he spoke:

"He helped me every day I was here…I love him."

As Tracy was completing his thoughts I could hear the plodding and clunking of our toddler in residence trying to make it up those steep back stairs. Eddie had obviously momentarily escaped his chaperone and was on his way up for a mid-morning adventure in that cluttered obstacle course of an attic that doubled as his Jungle Gym. I stood up and slipped past Tracy only to find Eddie was just two stairs from his goal. I held his hand to steady his final ascent. I greeted him at the top and he returned my greeting with a "Hi Tom."

"Does your mom know you're up here?" I asked, more to appear like a responsible adult than really concerned that Eddie's mother would be very worried.

"Tee-hee-hee." Eddie giggled in response, and then scurried past me towards a pile of clothing—indicating that I should have known better than to ask.

Tracy followed and soon he and Eddie were lost in the moment, oblivious to my presence. Tracy was a terrific playmate for Eddie because he could become lost in the moment just like a kid. I wondered if Tracy had found any consolation in our conversation and I worried whether I had cut him off prematurely when I rushed to help Eddie reach his goal. But I also knew my limitations and those of the circumstances in which we were immersed at the House of Mercy. No heart-to-heart talk, no matter how meaningful, was going to adequately address the larger mental health issues that Tracy would likely face for the rest of his life. My role was to make this small part of his long, hard pilgrimage just a tiny bit easier. I savored the playful spontaneity of Eddie and Tracy for a short interlude, and then I quietly slipped down the stairway toward the first floor. Productive work had now been abandoned and I was itching to find out more about how the House of Mercy ushered the poor and homeless into the next life.

At the bottom of the steps I met Eddie's tall, dark and lovely mother who was sternly calling for her son in a thick Caribbean accent. Feeling a little like Benedict Arnold, I directed her up the stairs where Eddie and Tracy played blissfully unaware that Eddie was about to be busted for running off and making a nuisance of himself. In truth, even when he was in the way of something important, he was rarely deemed a "nuisance" by anyone other than his mother. He was just so darned cute that he turned every interruption into comic relief. It was hard to come away from an encounter with Eddie feeling bad.

After betraying Eddie to his mother I darted into Grace's office, which was surprisingly abandoned—obviously in the rush to prepare for the funeral. Finding the office empty, I was about to exit and track down one of the staff to see if there was something I could do to help when my attention was drawn to the Wall of the Dead. I had seen it hundreds of times before and had even listened to the stories of the people pictured there, but I had never treated it with more than a passing curiosity until now. It dominated an entire wall of Grace's office and had even spilled haphazardly onto the adjacent wall as the years passed and the death toll mounted. On that wall pictures, poems, necklaces, trinkets and other personal effects were tacked up usually on top of the program from the funeral service. Every friend, guest, or benefactor of the House of Mercy who had passed on found a place on the Wall. Young and old, rich and poor, loved and abandoned, powerful and weak, all were well represented. I noticed for the first time that a shocking number of infants and toddlers adorned the Wall of the Dead. This, of course, reinforced and put flesh on those statistics I had heard so many times over the previous few years regarding the scandalously high infant and child mortality rates found in poor, minority, inner-city neighborhoods. I also noticed patterns of suicide and violent death that seemed entirely out of proportion to the size of the population.

I became completely immersed in the experience and began removing items to read about the individual's life and accomplishments, or to hold a precious item that embodied some special meaning for that person. With each item and every story I experienced a sense of loss and sorrow—a regret for having never had the chance to get to know that person. When I returned each item to the Wall I said a small prayer and felt oddly comforted by the personal contact I could sense with someone I had never met in the flesh—a sort of communion of the saints. What was this connection that could be experienced with people who no longer existed in this world, and who never had been encountered in this life? Were these merely emotional states inspired by idealized, artificial memories of someone? Or was the sensed connection something that, in some way, transcended a private emotional state and evidenced the existence of a spiritual bond that could somehow span the chasm between two very distinct worlds? Experiences like these always seem to bring us back to the most basic questions. Is faith truth, or just creative delusion?

"Oh, hi Tom. I didn't expect to see you in here." Grace's voice startled me as I spun to see her collecting things on her desk and picking up her purse. I responded while trying to regain my composure.

"Grace! God, you scared me. I was all wrapped up in the Wall of the Dead. I just couldn't stop looking at those faces and reading about their lives. I don't know what came over me." Grace paused, and looked in my eyes. A knowing smile formed on her lips as she said,

"Yeah, that happens to us all at one time or another."

"What do you mean?" I asked, puzzled by the idea that finding oneself lost in reflection was a common occurrence. Grace explained:

"I mean the Wall plays a very special role here at the House of Mercy. When the average person dies, their memory lives on with their children, grandchildren and friends. They die a physical death, but in the community they live on in the stories that are told and retold about them. The homeless normally lack family and communal ties, or those bonds have been broken by years of hard living on the street. When they die, they experience a double death if you will—they die physically and they die socially. In popular terms, they are both dead and gone. The Wall of the Dead is one of the ways we combat this assault on the dignity of the homeless. When we neglect the memory of these people, we also subtly deny their full humanity. Here we don't allow people to die like animals."

When Grace spoke from her heart it was always moving. Her conviction and passion were so transparent that I was caught momentarily off guard. What she said was brilliant. How she said it was divine. I wasn't sure how to respond so I asked a question instead:

"Well, are there other ways we uphold the humanity of the homeless when they die?"

"Look around. What are we doing right now?" She answered, stretching her arm out and around in a sweeping gesture. I wasn't sure where she was headed with this line of inquiry so I asked:

"What do you mean?"

"I mean, what have we been running around preparing for all morning?" She asked, leading me by the hand to my answer.

"The funeral," I said. Grace continued.

"Exactly. Do you know what the County does when a homeless person dies on the street and no one comes to claim the body?" I had no idea.

"No."

"They place it in the cheapest box they can find and unceremoniously drop it in an unmarked grave...They do almost as much for dead animals." Grace delivered the last sentence while fighting back the effects of strong emotion. I completed her thoughts.

"So the House of Mercy makes sure that every homeless and forgotten person who dies on our watch receives a funeral fit for a human being." Grace nodded, then, after composing herself, said:

"We're almost ready to go. Are you coming with us?"

"Yeah, Oh! Uh, Tracy was just talking to me upstairs and he really wants to say something at the funeral. Sweet Thing had a big impact on him." I said, simultaneously realizing how strange it sounded advocating that Tracy assume a public speaking role. Grace responded thoughtfully.

"You know, Tom, we try to give everyone a chance to express themselves, but Tracy could go off on one of his uncontrollable tangents and turn the funeral into a real circus."

"You're right, of course, but in his defense, he expressed himself clearly and concisely upstairs this morning, and it was all appropriate stuff that was heartfelt and touching. Maybe if we provide him with some clear boundaries he will be able to have his say without going off in all kinds of directions." I suggested.

"Let me talk to him." Grace requested.

After a thorough search of the house, I found Tracy in the back yard. When I told him that Sr. Grace wanted to talk to him about his possible speaking role at the funeral he became excited and started to straighten his cap and brush off his clothes. He then chuckled nervously, spun around and started walking toward the house. As he strode briskly toward the back door he glanced over his shoulder at me and paused, flashing a smile of appreciation in my direction. I smiled, waved and nodded in acknowledgement as he turned clumsily just in time to stumble up the back stairs and into the house.

As I walked down the driveway, I could see C.W. leaning with his outstretched arm against the jam of the sliding door of the van, looking a little frayed at the edges. When I approached he greeted me with a tired smile and a gesture with his right arm signaling an invitation to join the others in the van who would be attending the funeral at Our Lady of Perpetual Help (OLPH) parish. I ducked my head and stepped into the steel furnace crammed to capacity with hot and exasperated people, all of whom had obviously been waiting in their seats longer than they had anticipated. Some attempted to fan away the discomfort, while others closed their eyes and maintained a stoic stillness as if deep in contemplation. I wedged myself between Sr. Gloria and Prince in the back seat and waited with the others for Grace who was characteristically the last to depart or arrive. The rest of us resigned ourselves to this fact and became practiced at the virtue of patience.

When Grace appeared at the side door where the van was parked, she was carrying a package in her left hand and groping for her keys in her pocketbook with her right. C.W. took the package from her and placed it on the floor of the van as Grace gave him instructions on its care and handling. C.W. seemed to already know the identity of the recipient. Over her left shoulder Grace was lugging an enormous knit bag which held all of her files and paperwork. Only once in my ignorance had I ever volunteered to carry that forty-pound monstrosity, which was not merely heavy, but also awkward and unstable. A careless turn or preoccupied stoop could cause the bag and its loose-leaf contents to spray across what seemed to be acres. Because it had no rigid framework, the bag was equally difficult to refill after an accident—much like stuffing a plastic garbage bag with leaves. Being a seasoned veteran, Grace, of course, was a Kung Fu master when it came to handling both the heft and instability of this albatross.

When Grace found her keys, she told C.W. that she had changed her travel plans and would be driving her own car so that she could give a ride to Tracy and Elaine who had just shown up in her office asking if they could attend the funeral. When this brief huddle broke up, C.W. announced that the front seat was open. I turned to a reluctant Sr. Gloria, but before I could coax her into taking the seat the opportunity passed as others closer to the front vied for the throne. The trip to OLPH would only be a few minutes, which made me wonder: had we just started walking and not sat waiting in the van for half an hour, would we have arrived any later?

OLPH was a beautiful, twin steeple, Spanish colonial style church that had been recently restored to its original luster. This monumental anachronism stood tall and proud in the midst of the pervasive and rampant urban decay of Rochester's north side. Most of the parishioners were Sunday sojourners from other neighborhoods, drawn back to the parish of their childhood by a mixture of loyalty and nostalgia. Many were residents of northern suburbs whose families had lived in this neighborhood a generation or two ago. Those who did not fit into this significant demographic were likely to have been attracted to OLPH by its saintly pastor Fr. Neal Miller, who also just happened to be Sr. Grace's twin brother.

As far as twins go, Fr. Neal and Sr. Grace shared few superficial physical and character traits. However, at a deeper level, they shared a profound bond that witnessed to the same bond, I imagine, God has for us all. Both were nearing 60 years of age, but Sr. Grace had a youthful appearance emphasized by a smooth complexion and shoulder length blond hair. The love of God and humanity burned intensely and passionately in her. Grace's presence was incendiary in comparison to her brother's warm glow. Fr. Neal's appearance was more in conformity with his actual age—thinning white hair, a salt and pepper mustache and a waistline that had been enhanced by the care of a generous and talented flock. The glint in his eyes and a warm embrace always accompanied a greeting that made one feel perfectly welcome. The love of God and humanity radiated from him with constancy and deliberate care.

Fr. Neal had attended a couple of our Forum meetings and had just offered to host our meeting at his parish, given the transitional nature of our current location on Central Park and the unfinished status of our new location on Hudson Avenue. I had been to the parish rectory on a number of occasions with the rest of the House of Mercy staff to attend a community coalition that had been set up to address health issues for the poor and working classes. The leadership of this coalition was ideologically sophisticated, but lacked real practical commitment to social change. In other words, they enjoyed talking about strategies for social change, but rarely staged an executable social action. All of us, including Fr. Neal, were becoming frustrated by this comfortably eviscerated, intellectual leftism, which was looking more like an opportunity for liberal, middle-class narcissism, than a real chance for concrete change.

In our Forum meeting a few weeks back, I had carelessly referred to Fr. Neal's parish as an example of suburban absentee colonialism in the poor urban landscape. I apologized for my arrogance and callowness afterward, but instead of taking offence, Fr. Neal invited me to his next parish council meeting where he wanted me to help the leadership in his parish recognize the need to reach out to a neighborhood that had become progressively alien over the course of several decades of massive demographic migratory change.

As I greeted Fr. Neal before the funeral, he reminded me that the parish council meeting would be tomorrow night. A wave of anxiety rolled over me as he embraced me, and reassured me that "my message" was exactly what his parishioners needed to hear. This had the unintended effect of making me more nervous because until now I had been blissfully unaware that I was the bearer of *any* message that could be construed as uniquely my own.

As the funeral took shape around me, I sat in my pew ruminating on the possible content of a presentation to a parish council. Sr. Grace rehearsed an appropriate eulogy with Tracy as acolytes prepared the altar and pallbearers escorted the casket to the front of the church. Fr. Neal was vesting for the ceremony as the rest of the House of Mercy staff comforted and supported those who were mourning the passing of a good friend. Although the funeral was scheduled to begin at 11:00am, the time had apparently been conveniently translated into CP time because it was already twenty minutes past the hour and it would be another ten minutes before the actual liturgy would begin.

The liturgy itself was unremarkably conventional until it came to the homily. At this point Fr. Neal delegated the homily to those who wanted to come forward and eulogize the deceased. This, as well, was not an unusual practice, at least in my own experience of Catholic funeral services. One by one, people from the House of Mercy came to the microphone and shared stories about Sweet Thing. Each story made him present again in a different way as our imaginations reconstructed the scenes and characters that were being depicted in the narrative. Finally, Tracy and Sr. Grace came up to the pulpit to pay their public respects. Tracy delivered his rehearsed eulogy with minimal inappropriate laughter and bombast, and Sr. Grace was able to reign him in before he could begin pontificating on some tangential concern.

Sr. Grace then summarized our collective memories in a concise description of the man who had such a long and abiding presence in this close-knit community. Her words were touching even for those of us who had known him for only a few short months. At the House of Mercy, as with any good family, the dead live on in our collective memory as we tell and retell the stories of their lives. The funeral is only the first ritualized manifestation of this ongoing battle against the shameful forgetfulness known as social death. When homeless people suffer social death, they become symbols of our collective capacity to dehumanize the poor. If one believes that we human beings share a common dignity by virtue of our common humanity, then it logically follows that when the dignity of any person is threatened, then the dignity of every person is diminished. The House of Mercy did all of us a great service that day.

Sr. Grace concluded her remarks by recounting Sweet Thing's last words to her at his bedside in the hospital:

"He said, 'don't forget me baby.' And I said, 'don't be silly. How could we ever forget you?'"

Indeed, Sweet Thing will not be forgotten. To this very day, many years after his death, his picture hangs on that wall in that communion of saints at the House of Mercy, and relics of his life are regularly reassembled when we gather to put flesh on the dry bones of those who cry out to be remembered as human beings. Over time it has become clear to me that we need to regularly revisit the tombs of those who have passed through to make certain they are still empty.

Wandering

I stood, arms crossed, in the doorway to Sr. Grace's office-to-be, admiring my own handiwork with the carpet tiles I had just finished gluing to the floor. The cool, air-conditioned atmosphere now matched the freshly painted walls, thermal-pane windows, insulated doors, sliding closet doors, recessed light fixtures, complemented finally by the pristine carpet tiles. The contractors donating their time to renovate the new House of Mercy were less than reliable due to the fact that summer was their busy season—the time of year when they could make or break the business depending on how well they serviced paying customers. In spite of big promises we hadn't seen hair nor hide of them in weeks and our move-in date was upon us; so C.W., some volunteers and I were left to finish the floors, painting, trim and even some of the carpentry.

"Looks great!" C.W. said, as he perused the newly carpeted office. The hand he placed on my shoulder stuck to my tee-shirt and, like the rabbit in the Tar Baby story, he used his other gluey hand to try to disentangle the first one only to find both hands glued. Meanwhile I was trying to unfold my crossed arms only to realize my gluey hands stuck to the hairs on my forearms. In spite of the fact that we had more offices to tile, both of us knew we needed to clean up before going any further, so we made our way to the kitchen where a can of spirits would liberate us from this sticky situation.

"The whole place is looking great," I said, continuing C.W.'s line of thought. "Did you finish your office?"

"Yup, we just have Sr. Rita's office to finish and then we can start working on the second floor," C.W. replied.

"This place is going to be amazing!" I exclaimed. "The size of this building is going to make a lot of things, like food distribution and clothing storage, a whole lot easier."

"Well, don't be fooled by the size," C.W. retorted. "It's going to seem a whole lot smaller when it's filled with people."

I continued enthusiastically: "We could never fill this place, even if all the people from Central Park showed up at the same time."

C.W. patiently replied, "That's my point, Tom, we aren't on the fringes on little Central Park anymore. We are in the heart of a main north-south route at the center of poverty on the north side of the city. We are going to see a huge increase in the number of people coming to us. Heck, I've already had a taste of what's to come. Every day I talk to dozens of people asking me when we are going to open shop."

Still not sensing C.W.'s urgency, I interpreted his comments through my inexperienced rose-colored glasses. "Isn't that exciting! All those people drawn to our ministry even before we've moved in!"

C.W. was gentle in his correction. "Exciting?! Well, I guess you could look at it that way. You could also point to the fact that we are already woefully understaffed at Central Park and then the picture of multiplying your population by at least three looks a whole lot grimmer."

"Oh yeah, I hadn't thought about it in those terms," I said, as the weight of C.W.'s words began to sink in. C.W. confided:

"You know, I'm more than a little concerned that this move is going to completely overwhelm us. On the other hand, we have been dreaming about this kind of building at this sort of location for years. But now that the dream is almost a reality, I'm wondering if it's not going to end up being more like a nightmare."

What he had been trying to tell me was that our current level of hard work and sacrifice was only the tip of the iceberg. While we dissolved the carpet glue on our hands, I pondered how the relatively small staff at Central Park could absorb such a logarithmic increase in its service population. The excitement I felt concerning our move into a bigger, renovated building was becoming tempered by the realization that the change would involve far more than simply a change of venue. Many in the House of Mercy family would be left behind, either by choice, or by circumstances beyond anyone's control. Those who made the transition would find themselves among a sea of unfamiliar faces, most of whom would be struggling with poverty, homelessness, addiction, or some other form of desperation. Would the veterans accept and embrace the rookies? What patterns of violence, drug abuse, psychological disease, poverty and homelessness would be encounter at the center of Rochester's north side that we had not dealt with or even imagined while toiling at the margins of this reality?

When we had satisfactorily cleaned our hands, arms, legs and other contaminated body parts, we went right back to the task of gluing carpet tiles, this time in Sr. Rita's office. Arriving in the doorway with a stack of carpet tiles I noticed C.W. speaking to someone already in the room. Peering around C.W. I saw Sr. Rita unloading a couple of grocery bags filled with various medical supplies into what would become her new closet. She was accompanied by an elderly African American man known to everyone at the House of Mercy as Poppa Smurf. His nickname was derived from his resemblance to a popular cartoon character that shared the same general appearance, mannerisms and behavior patterns. Poppa Smurf stood about five and a half feet tall, had a dark complexion and carried a few more pounds than he probably should have. He was grumpy in a loveable way and spent his days at the House of Mercy flitting from one office to the next griping about anything and everything. He had expended much time and effort in his adult life trying to fight a dishonorable discharge from the armed services. The shame of this experience plagued him.

This morning he was having an oft-repeated argument with Rita about his drinking habits and his medication. He was an insulin-dependent diabetic, but frequently refused to take his medication and continued to drink alcohol, which, of course, was a suicidal recipe for disaster. He seemed to be tragically on a journey towards his own demise.

"Listen, after I get these bags unpacked we are going to get out of C.W.'s way and go into Grace's office and you are going to take your insulin injection in front of me." Rita asserted, as she stacked her supplies on the closet shelf.

"Aaawww, that's just snake venum. I ain't puttin' that crap in me. No way," came the mumbled retort from Poppa Smurf. Rita laughed briefly, then recomposed herself as she finished her shelving and grabbed Poppa Smurf by the hand saying:

"O.K. let's get out of here and let these guys get back to work. Now I am not going to let you go into shock right before my eyes this morning, so we are going into Grace's office and you will take your medication." Poppa Smurf muttered something unintelligible as they passed out of Sr. Rita's office and slipped into Sr. Grace's office next door.

C.W. and I got back to the sticky business of laying carpet tile. As we swept and prepared the concrete floor, I continued musing about these momentous changes coming upon the House of Mercy. My reflections naturally led back to those frequently rehearsed stories of our foundation.

The founding of the House of Mercy really began with the movement of the Spirit in the life of Sr. Grace Miller, who chose to join the religious order of the Sisters of Mercy because she was drawn to Catherine McAuley's vision that called for ministry to and solidarity with the poorest of the poor. It was this vision of the founder of the Sisters of Mercy which informed the initial inspiration and ongoing operational principles for the House of Mercy. After taking final vows in 1958, Grace returned to a teaching apostolate in a suburban Catholic grade school run by the order. Although she loved teaching, she was drawn almost instinctively toward the rawer realities of the inner city. In 1963 she requested a transfer to Mt. Carmel School located in the heart of Rochester's predominantly African American northern slums. Her request was granted and she spent the next two years immersing herself in this foreign culture. She was a quick study and soon earned the respect of the people in the neighborhood for her uncompromising advocacy on their behalf. The "poor" for her were not a problem to be solved, but rather real people with genuine dignity whose suffering was an offense to a compassionate God.

In July of 1964, riots erupted on the streets of Rochester in response to an incident in which police had arrested an African American man at a street festival for public drunkenness. High unemployment rates and desperately poor living conditions among Rochester's African Americans population had exacerbated frustration levels during that period of the City's history. These riots attracted national attention and soon an organization named FIGHT (Freedom, Independence, God, Honor, Today) emerged from these conflicts, which would deeply alter Rochester's political and social landscape for decades to come. Initially guided by the renowned community organizer, Saul Alinsky, FIGHT would eventually spawn many and various business and community organizations, some of which are still operating to this day.

In 1965, the burning issues for African Americans living in Rochester were jobs, education, voter registration, and political mobilization of the poor. These were the issues that FIGHT identified and organized to address. Their immediate and resounding successes were drawing the attention of Rochester's Catholic and Protestant clergy. An ecumenical coalition for urban ministry was developed, and out of these meetings the Catholic Diocese of Rochester formed an Office of Social Ministry under the directorship of David Finks.

Finks asked each religious community in the Rochester Diocese to send one representative to work with the newly formed Office of Social Ministry. When he approached the Sisters of Mercy they sent Sr. Grace because she was demonstrating such an obvious passion for social ministry, and because she already had experience collaborating with FIGHT on community development projects in her neighborhood. Her commitment to the Office for Social Ministry quickly became a full time occupation and for the next eleven years she worked hand-in-hand with FIGHT and other FIGHT-inspired organizations. In these years she nurtured and developed a confrontational style of direct action. She learned to trust and believe in the full participation of the poor and marginalized in their own liberation from oppressive forces. She became skilled at luring media attention and using that to her advantage. She became practiced in the art of street drama, aimed at embarrassing the rich and powerful, while highlighting the plight of the poor and desperate. She was loud; she was bold; she raged against injustice wherever she saw it. She was relentless because she believed God was relentless when it came to justice and love.

Grace won many friends on the street in those years and a few enemies in high places. In response to certain organizational changes at the Office for Social Ministry, she decided to leave the Office and pursue graduate study in theology at Catholic University in Washington, D.C. She spent the next year and a half in Washington and it was during this time that she was able to deepen her friendship with Fr. Charles E. Curran, a renowned theologian at Catholic University. Fr. Curran's friendship would be an ongoing comfort and support for Grace through the darkest and most difficult days of her ministry—days which loomed just around the next bend on her life path.

Grace left Catholic University in 1978 in order to take a position as co-pastor of St. Bridget's parish on the north side of Rochester. She worked with John Forni, a newly ordained priest, at this troubled inner city parish that boasted a congregation of thirty members, who were, for the most part, not members of the surrounding community. In fact, only two parishioners were African Americans from the immediate neighborhood. The congregation was so small that they chose not to use the church for Sunday mass, preferring instead to celebrate the liturgy in a large room in the parish hall—a decision that helped save on energy costs. Fr. John and Grace knew St. Bridget's couldn't survive in its present state as a tiny foreign enclave in an alien urban environment. Their plan was to go door-to-door, meet the people of the neighborhood, and invite them to experience the parish community. When their congregation doubled after their first evangelical effort, they decided to continue reaching out to their neighborhood in the same direct and personal way. A week before their first Christmas together, the parish distributed loaves of bread to nearby apartment complexes, each loaf accompanied by an invitation to Midnight Mass. Their newly formed gospel choir sang at that celebration to a congregation that filled St. Bridget's Church for the first time in decades. In addition to the gospel choir, a revived religious education program thrived during Grace's short tenure at St. Bridget's. The parish also became involved in social outreach to the community, eventually developing an especially effective job placement program.

St. Bridget's seemed to be on the rebound and the parish leaders were loved and respected by this resurrected congregation. However, Grace's unyielding advocacy for poor African Americans in Rochester, and her often brazen confrontations with political and ecclesial authorities had branded her as an undesirable in the eyes of many powerful Rochesterians. A conspiracy brewed to have her removed from her influential position at St. Bridget's. Since Sr. Grace and Fr. John worked closely as a team, Fr. John would need to be replaced by someone who would be less likely to defend Grace and more likely to view things from the perspective of her powerful enemies. They found such a candidate in Dozia Wilson, an African American priest who had been invited into the Rochester Diocese in order to serve the spiritual needs of a growing black Catholic population. While the changing of the guard superficially appeared to be a step in the right direction, Fr. Wilson and Grace soon discovered they did not see eye-to-eye on most issues, especially when it came to outreach, advocacy and service to the poor.

After a few months of perpetual strategic détente between their contrasting ministerial styles, Sr. Grace was beginning to question her role at St. Bridget's. She decided to take a week off and journey to the countryside to discern the proper orientation of her life and ministry. When she returned to mass the next Sunday she was asked to leave by Fr. Wilson. She reluctantly complied with the request; but when a large contingent of parishioners approached Grace entreating her to return as co-pastor she decided to return to mass that next Sunday. At that liturgy Fr. Wilson called the police to have Grace physically removed from the premises. The scandal was too public to go unnoticed by the media, and when the story hit the press the Bishop threatened to close the parish if Sr. Grace refused to yield. For the sake of the parish community, Grace resigned as co-pastor.

The next five years of Grace's life she describes as her "dark night of the soul." After leaving St. Bridget's she spent time at various retreat centers in Syracuse, NY, Kentucky, and Maryknoll, NY. She also worked in Harlem for a few months thinking she might relocate there to be with the poor. Eventually, she returned to Rochester and for a year worked at a job in a private social service agency known as the Baden Street Center. Part of her job was to find temporary housing for the homeless in the neighborhood. To the consternation of her boss, she frequently allowed the homeless to sleep on the couch in her office if she couldn't find an immediate placement. One day when she was out of the office, her boss found a homeless man sleeping on her couch. He filled a glass with water and threw it in the man's face telling him to get out of the office. When the startled man became angry, the director called the police to have him removed. Afterwards, when Grace confronted the director about his behavior, he fired her for insubordination.

Once again her dismissal created a public uproar that was covered by the local media. As a result, Grace became blacklisted in the Rochester area because of the bad press and a reputation for making waves wherever she went. Try as she might, Grace could not find a permanent position at any parish or agency for the next five years. On occasion she was able to teach in public schools as a substitute, and she almost went to Nicaragua with the organization, Witness for Peace. However, these tasks were not her real passion. Meanwhile, job interview after job interview resulted only in unemployment, and grant proposal after grant proposal went unfunded. Ultimately, Grace found herself wandering in a dry and featureless spiritual desert, in need of refreshment, but with little clear direction regarding where to turn to slake her thirst.

In the fall and early winter months of 1984, Grace began picking up homeless people she found on the street late at night, taking them to nearby shelters. When she arrived, more often than not, the shelters would not take the people in for various reasons. Many shelters claimed they had reached their capacity; others would only accept individuals who had been referred by another agency; still others would not accept anyone who was inebriated or under the influence of an illegal substance. A number of the people Grace picked up had been blacklisted from every shelter for inappropriate behavior. She also noticed that all of the shelters ejected the homeless back out onto the streets on or before 7am. On certain dark, frigid, mid-winter mornings this seemed like very harsh and inhumane treatment to Grace. One subzero January night, she picked up three men and called around to every shelter in Rochester to try to find them a place to stay. All of the shelters refused to take them in. Finally, Grace drove them to one of the shelters and demanded the men be taken in out of the cold. Two of the three found a place in the shelter. The third stayed with Grace's brother, Fr. Neal, at Our Lady of Perpetual Help parish.

Grace's experiences with the Rochester homeless shelters were the catalyst for what would become the House of Mercy. In response to her frustration with the current system of homeless services, she wrote a proposal for a storefront homeless outreach in February of 1985. She submitted the proposal to the provincial board of the Sisters of Mercy for approval in March, and by April her project was approved with $20,000 of startup funding. In what seemed to be a mere instant, her dark night of the soul had ended, and the vast desert that had vexed her during so many years of wandering had been transformed into a refreshing oasis.

On October 1, 1985, the doors opened at the first House of Mercy in a small rented single family home on Central Park Avenue. On that first day, the only furniture in the house was a donated steel desk and a wobbly swivel chair. That morning Grace ordered telephone service and waited until the installer showed up so she could orient him to the building and show him where she wanted phone jacks to be located. Grace then bid him goodbye and left him so she could take food to some families. When she returned, there was no sign of the technician or his contracted handiwork. When she called the phone company she found out he had driven off in a panic when Grace left him alone because he was afraid of the people in the neighborhood.

Such were the early days at the House of Mercy which found Sr. Grace struggling like the rest of the poor to meet even the most basic needs. Fear, prejudice, ignorance and hatred made it difficult to find volunteers and coworkers. Nonetheless, on that same fateful day in October 1985, a newly professed Sister of Mercy, Rita Lewis, visited the nascent House of Mercy which was the last stop on a tour of the ministries available through her order of nuns in the Rochester area. As she was leaving she turned to Sr. Grace and the other sisters accompanying her and said, "Now *this* is the work of Catherine McAuley." This would be the first of many visits for Rita over the next couple of years, and in 1987, she would be the first to join Sr. Grace on staff.

By the time Sr. Rita joined the staff, the House of Mercy had outgrown the tiny one story building on Central Park. In April of 1987 the House of Mercy moved across the street to a larger two family, two-story structure that could better accommodate the burgeoning population. What began as a ministry to a few hundred per month, had progressively grown to one serving over one thousand on a monthly basis. The owner of the building had invited St. Grace to move the ministry onto his property, and the House of Mercy enjoyed very good relations with the new landlord. However, when the landlord was murdered a few years later, his daughter inherited the property and fell behind on the repairs and the taxes.

A short time afterward, Sr. Rita joined the staff, and Sr. Grace's cousin, Gloria Ruocco, also a Sister of Mercy, came on board. Gloria immediately took over the enormous task of coordinating the Christmas program that distributed gifts and food to poor and homeless families. When Christmas was over, Gloria took over the tutoring program for school-age children and the summer school that helps children in struggling families get a head start on the upcoming school year. She also helped people in the neighborhood get the tax rebates on their rent to which they were entitled.

One day, about a year after Rita and Gloria joined the staff, Rita approached Grace and said, "You know, we really should have a man on the staff." Her comment arose out of the experience of yet another violent incident in which Rita and the rest of the staff felt powerless and overwhelmed. They feared that it would only be a matter of time before the violence and chaos was directed at one of them, resulting in serious injury, or even death. In response to this pressing need the House of Mercy would eventually hire Charles W. Earsley, better known as C.W. He had been homeless himself for a short period of time after his marriage dissolved due to the deteriorating mental health of his wife. When he first came on staff he was still technically homeless since he was living in a room at a friend's house. C.W. was hired after having been a volunteer at the House of Mercy for more than a year and he already had earned a reputation as a responsible, reliable, hard-working member of the team. C.W. also earned the respect of virtually everyone in the neighborhood, and his word carried a unique credibility and authority among the guests at the House of Mercy. He had walked in their shoes, yet, in so many ways, he had also risen above the desperate circumstances of his past and became a recognizable leader in the community. Humble yet confident, strong but good natured, serious yet good humored, C.W. combined qualities of wisdom and inner strength in such a way as to transform what should have been a mundane workman's position into a genuine leadership role.

"C.W....C.W.!" The voice of Slim rose as he tried to get C.W.'s attention. I snapped out of my reflections on the origins of the House of Mercy and looked up to see the sweat rolling down the face of this tall, dark, African American man leaning with outstretched arm against the far wall. Slim was about fifty years old, but had the body of an eighteen year old weight lifter. He was a quiet man with a wry sense of humor, who was a fixture of sorts at the House of Mercy. Unfortunately, at this time in his life it was difficult to motivate Slim to do anything except take more drugs. With surprise C.W. responded:

"Yeah...hey, Slim, look at you all sweated up like you've been workin' all afternoon."

Slim laughed, scratched his head and muttered: "I don't know what got into me. I'll have to take the rest of the year off or somethin'." We all had a good laugh.

"What's up?" C.W. queried.

"We got the desks, chairs and cabinets you ordered sir." Slim said, feigning an inferior demeanor. C.W. strode toward the door, and putting his arm on Slim's shoulder, he directed him out of the room saying,

"I'll go with you. Tom and I just finished the carpet tiles in Gracie and Rita's office. That's Grace's office and we were just in Rita's..." C.W.'s voice trailed off as they meandered toward the front of the building and I tuned them out as I returned to the task of laying the last few carpet tiles. Before they were completely out of earshot I heard Slim exclaim,

"Damn, C.W., you all sticky!"

None of us suspected it at the time, but Slim had just begun a long journey toward sobriety that would come to fruition six years later at Farbridge House, a satellite outreach of the House of Mercy to chemically dependent individuals seeking to get off alcohol and drugs.

A few minutes later Slim and C.W. returned straining under the weight of Sr. Grace's desk. I had just laid the last carpet tile in Rita's office so I walked over to the doorway to observe the movers, all the while enjoying that satisfying feeling one gets after completing a long and hard job. To my surprise, C.W. and Slim were trailed by Tracy who was carrying a couple of chairs. For a number of reasons, not the least of which was his propensity to jabber on meaninglessly for long periods of time, Tracy was not high on anyone's volunteer list. I concluded that there must have been a labor shortage on Central Park that afternoon. As he passed, Tracy confided:

"Hide brotha', they gonna make slaves outta all of us…even you."

"Tracy…we need the chairs in *here*." C.W. commanded.

"Yeah, yeah, yeah, I hear ya boss." Tracy said with a chuckle. Then as he entered Grace's office he exclaimed in a surprised tone:

"Hey this is nice!"

Slim seconded Tracy's praise. "Yeah C [short for C.W.], with offices like these nobody's gonna know where they at. They gonna think they on the set of the Wizard of Oz or somethin'."

"Don't you worry. I give this place a month—two at tops. After that," C.W. clapped his hands to emphasize his point. "things will be back to their normal smelly, grimy, messy, crazy state of affairs." C.W.'s fatalistic comment rang true for all of us and within two months his words would prove prophetic.

We spent the rest of the afternoon moving desks, chairs, file cabinets and other office furniture from Central Park to the new location on Hudson Avenue. I was paired with Tracy for the afternoon, which I really didn't mind because I had discovered that if I interrupted him and kept asking directive questions I could almost keep him on topic. Nonetheless, it was a tiring exercise because I had to stay ever vigilant and focused lest I let one of Tracy's tangents gain momentum. Inevitably the tangents would win the day and Tracy would be off pontificating in his own little world seemingly oblivious to his surroundings. It struck me that afternoon how Tracy's disease had trapped him in a permanent mental state of wandering. I wondered if all that wandering could ever result in peace for Tracy—a goal, an end, a resting place.

The next day was a Saturday and the move from Central Park was in full swing with everyone involved in one way or another—even if it meant, for some, only moving themselves. All of the large furniture items had been taken care of the day before and my own files and office supplies had been moved last night into my new air-conditioned space on the second floor. Decked with fresh paint, carpeted floors and new light fixtures, with a window looking out onto the second floor deck, I paused and perused my new location. Oddly enough, instead of excitement and satisfaction I felt discomfort and guilt. I wondered what I had done to deserve all this luxury and the obvious answer was not nearly as much as the rest of the staff, which kept nagging at me as

I tried vainly to properly appreciate my brand new digs. Mercifully, my guilt trip was detoured by practical consideration.

"Tom…Tom?" A small, nasal voice that sounded like Grace's was coming out of a speaker, but I was having difficulty locating the source. Finally, I noticed it was coming from the phone on my desk.

"Yeah, hi, hello?!" I chanted at the phone, but there was no answer. Realizing I was not being heard by those at the other end, who were by now talking among themselves wondering if I was in my office or somewhere else, I picked up the receiver and answered.

"Hello?"

"Oh, hi Tom ! Isn't this great. I love these new phones," Grace replied, sounding playful and perky.

"Oh yeah," I said, "But I think they're more clever than I am."

"You can say that again," Grace bellowed, "I just got mine to work after twenty minutes of fidgeting. The DND button was lit. Do you know what DND means?" I didn't have a clue. Grace continued without my input. "It means 'do not disturb,'" Grace chuckled. "Fat lot of chance I have not being disturbed around this place. Anyway, beware of the DND button. It pretty much shuts you down."

"I'll try to steer clear of that one," I said as I scanned the dozen or so buttons arrayed across the face of my phone for the one marked 'DND.'

"Anyway, believe it or not I didn't call you just to tell you about the DND button," she said, as she chuckled once again. "I was wondering if you could help C.W. move into his new apartment upstairs. I have Carrie Goings in my office and she said she'd be happy to help."

Relieved to have a mission that would temporarily take me from my newfound source of guilt I answered:

"Sure, I'd be happy to help."

"Great! I think C.W. is out front with the van. I'll send Carrie out to meet you," Grace concluded as she hung up.

C.W, Carrie and I spent the rest of the morning packing and unpacking the van filled with C.W.'s personal effects. C.W. was living in a low rent apartment complex where Tricky Dick and Slim also resided. He was moving into a large one room studio apartment on the second floor of the new House of Mercy where he would pay no rent, but would be on call virtually twenty four hours a day. Nevertheless, from C.W.'s perspective, this was clearly a step in the right direction. As he saw it, he was already dealing with a number if the regulars at the House of Mercy on a twenty-four hour basis at his current abode. Why not live for free and take on the whole Magilla? Carrie and I were in no position to argue.

Carrie was a short African American woman in her early thirties with a solid build and a light complexion. I had only known her a few days, but already I could tell she was sincere and always aiming to please. From her efforts that day she proved she was a hard worker and she liked to converse while packing and carrying boxes. Over the course of our numerous trips to and from C.W.'s old and new apartments, Carrie outlined her touching and painful story. She had been brought up in an abusive home with a father who was physically and sexually aggressive, and a mother who was too passive and fearful to intervene. She had two children at the time, one of whom was likely the product of an involuntary liaison with her father. She left home when she was in her teens for obvious reasons and fell into a life of drug abuse and prostitution.

I had heard from Sr. Grace that Carrie was a loving mother in spite of her background and drug use. However, after repeated drug related offences the courts took her children away when she was only twenty-four and the children were six and seven. The children were placed in foster care against their will. Carrie was devastated by the court order and ended up living on the streets, no longer concerned with maintaining a household if its only purpose was to sustain herself. Eventually Carrie made her way to the House of Mercy where Sr. Grace was advocating with the court system to have Carrie's children returned to her. At this juncture they were battling just to establish visitation rights. Her eldest son, Darnell, had run away from foster care several times in an attempt to be reunited with his mother. Carrie, in the meantime, was spending her nights sleeping on a sofa at the House of Mercy, yearning for the day she would be able to hold her beloved children again.

Like an epiphany it struck me how Carrie was like Tracy, who was like Slim, who was like Poppa Smurf, who was like C.W., who, in turn, was like the whole House of Mercy and me. In one way or another everyone with whom I came into contact that summer seemed to be in some state of wandering—somewhere between exodus and occupation—between Egypt and the Promised Land.

In Communion with the Poor

I never imagined that seventy-two degrees could be so cold, but there I was shivering violently sitting in my new desk chair cursing the very same air conditioning unit that I praised as my savior only a few short weeks before. It was late August, but it was still quite warm and muggy on any given day, so wearing long pants and a long sleeve shirt would have made my bike ride to work unbearable. It was clear I would have to abandon my plans to sit at my desk and prepare the next Forum meeting in order to get up and do something a little more active. I had tried calisthenics earlier in the day when I felt chilled just before lunch, but I became too embarrassed when on my way up from one of my toe touches I caught sight of Sr. Gloria standing in the hallway, arms folded, staring at me with a bemused look on her face. Startled, I attempted to explain myself in halting starts and stops, but this just compounded my humiliation. Sr. Gloria gave me a final glance and a smirk of disbelief as she disappeared into her office saying,

"Don't worry Tom; only God and I know your secret." I had nothing for a comeback and, in any case, I make it a policy never to try and one up a smart-aleck nun—years of life in community usually have prepared them to win such battles.

I made my way down the back steps that I had finished painting and carpeting just a few days before. At the bottom of the stairs was the new kitchen which was teaming with volunteers and guests busily gabbing and laughing. I was tuning into the conversation in the kitchen as I reached the last few steps and the topic of conversation was Poppa Smurf who had passed away last week. His funeral had been a major event at the House of Mercy just a few days ago. I paused at the bottom of the stairs to hear his closest friends tell stories of humor and sadness, strength and frailty, passion and death. These individuals constituted Poppa Smurf's inner circle at the House of Mercy since he spent a good deal of his time sitting on a stool "shootin' the shit" with the kitchen staff. Amidst this touching re-membering of Poppa Smurf a young African American woman named Eleanor, who regularly volunteered in the kitchen, recounted her last conversation with him on a visit to the hospital the day before he died.

"I started cryin', like I always do, cause Poppa was bein' so brave." She said. Pausing to compose herself, she continued. "Then he said, 'girl, why you cryin'? Don't you know the old gotta move on to make room for the young?'"

Eleanor choked out the last few words before she broke out in tears. Those gathered quietly affirmed the semitments expressed in Poppa Smurf's wisdom with nods of their heads and muffled amens. As I slipped around the corner and began to descend the basement stairs, I wondered if the old House of Mercy would make room for the young and new one that was being born on Hudson Avenue. Could the old and used up ways die to themselves so new and vibrant ones could have the freedom and space to develop and grow? Time would tell, but one thing was certain, dying is rarely as peaceful a process as most of us would like to believe. Processes and policies have a life of their own, and like living creatures, they struggle to maintain and reassert themselves even when their time has clearly come and gone. The House of Mercy was in that unique moment which most dynamic systems experience at one point or another in their existence—the new and the old were in a battle for supremacy and the outcome of this skirmish would determine the future viability of the organization. Would the old yield to the new? Would the new learn from the old? The weeks that followed would test the limits of these questions and ultimately result in an answer that would secure a future for the House of Mercy in a series of innovative ministries that were, at the same time, rooted in its founding principles and traditions.

Turning right again at the landing, I descended another short flight of stairs which led to the concrete floor of our enormous basement. Here I knocked on a locked makeshift door that had been erected to protect the donated food, clothing and household items from falling into the hands of would-be street entrepreneurs.

"Yeah, who is it?" Called Mrs. Washington, apparently from a room at quite a distance from the door.

"It's me, Tom O'Brien," I yelled back.

"Alright, I'm coming," she muttered in an exasperated voice just loud enough for me to hear. I felt guilty now for interrupting her because, in truth, I was just killing time and warming up the joints. Nonetheless, I was not about to reveal this to her. I heard her fidget with the lock on the knob and then slide the deadbolt with a snapping sound. Mrs. Washington's head popped out momentarily as she identified me and then examined the hall and stairway for potential interlopers. Then she swung the door open and motioned me in, closing and locking the door behind me.

"You want to see C.W.?" She asked.

"Why is he down here?" I said, surprised he wasn't running the errands he told me he would be busy with all afternoon.

"No," Mrs. Washington retorted. "I just thought that if you were looking for *him*, then I'd tell you you ain't gonna find him down here cause' he's gone for the whole afternoon."

"That's OK, I just came down to help out with the food," I said, hoping I wouldn't be indentured into the most disdainful task of sorting and hanging clothing. The food was just heavy, while the clothing was likely to be repellent to one or more of the senses, and often one couldn't reliably predict which bag or garment would be revolting until it was too late to insulate oneself. Mrs. Washington laid it all out for me:

"Well, a whole bunch of boxes of canned stuff came in on a truck today. It's at the bottom of the front stairs and needs to be hauled off to a back room. But there's a lot of boxes there, and they're heavy, let me tell you! C.W. was going to get some of the men volunteers to help move that stuff tonight. You sure you don't want to help us out with the clothing? We have lots to unbox and hang."

"Uh, no. We'll probably get more done if we divide our efforts," I said, trying to sound like I wasn't rationalizing my way out of sorting clothes.

"OK. Knock yourself out. I'll be in here if you need anything else," Mrs. Washington said as she ducked into the large basement room where she and a couple of others were hanging donated clothing from exposed pipes running along the first floor joists overhead. In addition to retrieving the occasional yucky piece of clothing, one could encounter all kinds of hard-to-kill insects or disturb decades-old asbestos insulated pipes during an average clothing-sort shift. I bade my adieus with a spring in my step feeling like I had dodged at least one bullet that day. However, when I rounded the corner the enormity of the task which lay ahead of me stopped me in my tracks. Piled from floor to ceiling, in a twenty by thirty foot area were boxes of canned fruit, vegetables, soup and beans. A quick estimate put the number of boxes at well over one thousand. A brief experiment told me I wouldn't be able to carry more than one at a time. Suddenly there appeared an upside to the task of sorting yucky clothing. My misguided sense of pride won out against my more practical instincts that afternoon as I dove into the Herculean task like an ant after yet another rubber tree plant. Never had we received so much food. Of course, at our other locations we would never have had the capacity to accept a shipment of this size. Everything seemed to be increasing except the number of staff people, and on that afternoon, really for the first time, I was faced concretely with the very real problems of this logarithmic increase in demand for our services.

When the House of Mercy first opened its doors in 1985 on Central Park Avenue, it was serving about six hundred people per month. Those numbers gradually increased so that by the time they moved to the second location across the street, they were serving over one thousand people in a month. When they vacated that location five years later, the number had risen to two thousand. According to C.W.'s first counts at the new location on Hudson Avenue, the client population had tripled in size and he was projecting that we would soon be serving an average of six thousand people per month. That amounted to a ten-fold increase in the course of eight years of operation. Suddenly, C.W.'s anxieties were becoming all too clear. Divide the number of boxes of food stacked before me by ten and the task would become difficult, but accomplishable; however, as it stood, I could barely put a dent in that pile of boxes even though I spent the better part of three hours lugging them across a rough and uneven basement floor. In the end, I sat huffing and puffing on one of the boxes, feeling unfulfilled and defeated by my effort.

I could hear Mrs. Washington and her volunteers wrapping up their efforts for that day in the clothing distribution center. Mrs. Washington was thanking each of them as they collected their things and headed upstairs. Like so many of our veteran volunteers, Mrs. Washington was being forced to adjust her style of service. At Central Park she worked alone most days. On Hudson Avenue she was rapidly becoming more of a supervisor for a workforce of three to six volunteers. Her people skills were unpolished, though adequate enough for the task at hand. As she turned the light out and closed the door behind her, she paused, holding her breath in silence, then walked in my direction, probably attracted by the unexpected light in this part of the basement.

"Oh, honey, you still here?! Damn you look all nasty and tired! I told you you should have worked with us. We're tired, but we're still respectable," she said with a brief percussive laugh at the end. I smiled and gave an exhausted laugh saying,

"You were right on that account."

"You'll know better next time. Helping Mrs. Washington is a lot like helping yourself. I'll work you, but never too hard," she said, sounding like the voice behind those slogan-laden public service announcements. It was an easy sale that afternoon.

"I'll never doubt you again, Mrs. Washington," I said, dropping my head in my hands, elbows resting on my knees.

"That's right…Now get up and let's get out of here. We've both had enough of this basement for one day," she said, snapping the light off as I passed by her in the doorway.

It was the end of the day for Mrs. Washington, but I had promised to meet that evening with a special task force that had been formed in order to address the issue of the State's plan to use a fingerprint identification system. This system was purportedly aimed at reducing fraud in the welfare system; however, many of the poor and their advocates were skeptical that such a system would accomplish much more than effectively stigmatizing welfare recipients as criminally dishonest. Most of the people who were meeting tonight had been part of a coalition that was meeting at Fr. Neil's parish. They had become disillusioned by the diluted and ineffectual nature of this coalition's approach, so they were hoping to start their own more focused social action committee dealing primarily with the fingerprinting issue. In truth, this group consisted largely of people who were already in the House of Mercy's Forum, which had become known as the Rochester People's Forum over the course of the summer. To me, the newly forming group seemed like a duplication of our efforts in the Forum, so my enthusiasm for this evening's task force was tempered by my attitude.

After saying goodbye to Mrs. Washington, I wandered around the House of Mercy only to find it eerily empty. No one was in the kitchen. A few people I didn't recognize were watching television in the dining room. The reception desk was abandoned, although there were a few people sitting on the couches, apparently waiting to meet with a staff member about problems they were facing. I walked down the front steps into the huge living room and found only Carrie and

Slim watching television, with two other men asleep on the couches at the other end of the room. Carrie and I exchanged casual greetings and Slim nodded in my general direction, never taking his eyes off the daytime talk show that was examining the foibles of some poor pathetic freak who apparently felt an overwhelming need for too much attention. I left Slim and Carrie so they might continue to savor these sideshow delights in peace. Walking across the newly tiled linoleum floor I made my way to the conference room that doubled as a tutoring room, which also housed a small library and a large chalkboard. Through the windows I could see Sr. Gloria sitting at the conference table tutoring two girls and a boy. The children seemed to be about the age of fourth or fifth graders. They had just started back to school a few days ago and Sr. Gloria was doing her best to get them off to a good start. Sr. Grace had asked for the windows to be installed between the main lobby and the conference room so the guests could witness and be inspired by the educational ministries that went on within. Although the windows could invite distractions, especially from guests who were drunk or high, this panoramic view into the conference room had already motivated a number of neighborhood parents to send their children here for tutoring with Sr. Gloria.

I stood in the lobby examining Gloria's face for signs of frustration, exhaustion, or apathy. She had already worked a long day and almost everyone else in Rochester was on his or her way home for the evening. Most of her peers were gearing up for retirement, if they had not already jumped ship and moved to some sunny climate. Tirelessly, patiently, and lovingly, Sr. Gloria addressed their questions and explained the concepts these children needed to be successful in their class the next day. I reflected for a moment on Sr. Gloria's dedication to these unsung tasks and wondered if the enormity of her contributions would ever by recognized. In the next moment I realized that the relative anonymity of her ministries was part of a life she chose, and that this was probably the way she would prefer to be remembered.

Sr. Gloria's hand waving brought me out of my reverie. After getting my attention she motioned an invitation to enter the room. It had not been my intention to interrupt her tutoring with my aimless afternoon wandering, but she seemed insistent so I reluctantly went in.

"Hi Sr. Gloria," I said, with an apologetic smile.

"Hi Tom! Come on in and meet Towanda, Modina, and Charlie," she said, putting her hand on the shoulder or head of each of the children she was introducing.

"Hi everyone. It looks like you're working hard tonight. You know you have the best tutor in all of Rochester," I said, trying to hasten by retreat while in some way making up for the intrusion by plugging Sr. Gloria's tutoring ministry. She responded in a characteristically humble way:

"Well, I don't know about that."

"Do you three normally receive tutoring together?" I asked the students.

"Charlie and I usually work together," Towanda responded. "Modina is going to start going to the Breakfast Club tomorrow."

"The Breakfast Club, what's that?" I asked, puzzled by the reference to this unknown entity. Sr. Gloria jumped in with the answer:

"Haven't you heard? It started the other day. Some of the men who sit on the curb out front noticed that some of the children were going to school hungry. A few days ago those men and a few of the women guests started making the kids breakfast in our kitchen. It's a really nice breakfast with bacon, eggs, toast and juice."

"You mean they just started this up spontaneously—no staff involvement at all?" I asked a little incredulously.

"Oh yeah, everyone thinks it's a great outreach. Grace loves it. She thinks it will be great PR for the House of Mercy," Gloria explained, in her gentle, but energetic way.

I was more than intrigued by news of this edifying outpouring of concern and generosity on the part of a group of people who had more than enough to occupy themselves just taking care of their own immediate needs. I wanted to hear Sr. Grace's interpretation of this new ministry of the poor so I promptly dismissed myself, offering farewells to Sr. Gloria, Charlie, Modina and Towanda, and slipped quietly out the door through which I had entered moments ago. As I exited I could hear Sr. Gloria redirecting her students to the homework topic at hand,

In the dusky late afternoon illumination that cast a shadowy light in the lobby, I navigated the small stairway that led up and away from the lobby and into the northwest corner of the building where the staff offices were located. I passed a lavatory on the left and C.W.'s office on the right. The last door on the right was Grace's new office, which was at the end of an adjacent hallway leading to the reception area. I knocked, because at this time of day she kept her door locked. Although she would probably have been safe on this subdued afternoon, on most days needy guests and neighbors would have inundated her were she to carelessly leave her door ajar.

C.W. answered my knock.

"Oh, hi Tom. Come on in."

"Hi C.W., how did the afternoon go?" I asked as I closed and locked the door behind me.

"That's what Sr. Grace and I are talking about. The Food Bank informed me that they can't deliver the amount of food we requested and that we're going to have to go and pick up anything that exceeds one of their vanloads," he informed me, sitting down in one of the desk chairs that littered the space in front of Sr. Grace's desk. I responded as I sat in a chair across from him,

"But we don't have a van or truck to pick up that much food regularly."

"Exactly. We could use Tim's truck, but we would only have access to it now and again. Gracie's on the phone with the Food Bank now…" C.W.'s voice trailed off as Sr. Grace held up her hand gesturing for us to keep things down a bit. For the next forty-five minutes C.W. and I witnessed Grace's persistence as she argued our case with the managers of the Food Bank. She appeared to have negotiated some kind of compromise as she hung up the phone and reported the results.

"Well, they're going to drop off two vanloads of food per week rather than only one, but I still don't think that will be enough according to what C.W. was telling me about the demand for food at this place— it's huge by comparison to Central Park!"

"That's right, but I'm impressed you finagled two deliveries out of them. If I'm not mistaken, we'll be the only agency in Rochester that gets that kind of service out of them," C.W. said, congratulating Grace for her negotiating prowess.

"Thanks C.W. Hi Tom, I haven't seen you all day." Grace said as we both stood up to greet one another with a hug.

"I've been in the cellar carrying boxes of food all afternoon," I said, in a slightly disgusted tone as I sat back in my chair. C.W. chimed in:

"You didn't have to do that! I had a crew lined up for that job. They were going to make short work of that pile tomorrow."

"Don't worry," I said, reassuringly. "There are plenty of boxes left to move. You can barely tell I was there."

After a brief silence Sr. Grace changed the topic:

"I'm really concerned about this new place and it's not just the additional work and the many new faces. I don't like this building. I know that in a lot of ways this place fulfills so many of our long-term dreams, but somehow it's all too big, too new, too sterile. It isn't homey and inviting like Central Park. I'm not sure the people feel welcome."

"I think that's going to change all too soon Sr. Grace," C.W. said in a thoughtful tone. "We've already seen the guests taking ownership in ways we never anticipated."

"Yeah, like what about this so-called 'Breakfast Club'? Sr. Gloria was just telling me about it before I cam into your office," I said, finally bringing the conversation around to the issue I had originally come into Grace's office to discuss.

"Isn't that something!" Grace exclaimed, switching her mood instantaneously from worried to excited. "And you know, none of the staff knew about it until two or three days after it had already become a House of Mercy institution. Of course, I never would have found out about it if someone hadn't told me, since I don't get here until two or three in the afternoon."

"And you don't leave until two or three in the morning," C.W. added by way of a footnote. Grace continued.

"It was about a week ago that C.W. first realized that the homeless men who sit on the curb out in front on Hudson Avenue had started inviting the neighborhood kids who were waiting for their school bus to join them for breakfast. The kids started coming earlier and earlier, and now we feed about a dozen of them. The homeless guys do it all. And now these kids, who used to go to school hungry, have a hearty meal served family style. It's the poor feeding the poor. That's what we're all about—hospitality!"

We continued to talk about many things that evening. We talked until the coalition meeting began in the conference room. Had it not been for Rita bringing home a bucket of chicken, none of us would have eaten dinner that night. Thankfully, the coalition decided to simply meld with the Forum in order to avoid a duplication of efforts on the part of a majority of those in attendance. On the way home that night I was feeling relieved about that decision, but my thoughts were more occupied by the breakfast ministry. I decided I would arrive a few hours early the next morning so I could witness for myself the ministry of the 'Breakfast Club'.

Summer was clearly over in Rochester and my way to work was becoming cooler and less amenable to commutation by bicycle. Not only was the weather more hostile, but Hudson Avenue itself was a busy, often chaotic, thoroughfare, which was frequented by harried and hurried drivers who could be careless and rude. Some intersections were a jumble of cars, bikes, and pedestrians, all trying to assert their own agenda with little or no consideration for the customs and habits of others, or even the laws of the land. These pockets of commuter anarchy were both attractive, due to their ability to manufacture surprises, and repulsive, due to their inherent danger. This morning I would negotiate those intersections with the usual mixture of exhilaration and fear, wondering how much further into the autumn season I could push my bicycle commute.

I approached the large, white stucco, two-story, storefront that was now the new location for the House of Mercy. Darting across Hudson Avenue at an opportune moment, I parked and locked my bike on a signpost and greeted some of the men on the curb. Eventually, I inquired about breakfast and I was informed that the first group of children was already inside eating. Apparently the children arrived in two shifts because it had become too popular to attempt to feed them all at once. I used the main entrance through an alley on the side of the building and made my way upstairs past an empty reception desk and into the dining room.

What I saw that morning could be interpreted on a number of different levels. On a strictly objective level, it was a rather ordinary breakfast being served to a dozen children of varying ages by five unremarkable adults. Some of the children talked and laughed, while others silently ate hungrily. Some of the adults cooked, while others served or ate themselves. The food, the setting and the people involved were all humble and easily dismissed as insignificant.

However, when I looked at this thoroughly ordinary scene, I couldn't help but see much more. Images from the Christian Scriptures persistently intruded into the interpretations of the events unfolding before me. I couldn't resist the image of Jesus feeding the multitudes—how so much good had come from those with so little. This image was then replaced by a vision of Hudson Avenue as a contemporary manifestation of the Road to Emmaus—where Jesus became known in the breaking of the bread. These images continued to morph into others, and I saw the poor widow contributing a penny to the Temple treasury—how out of their need these homeless people had contributed what little they had. The final vision was of the earliest Christian communities in which the disciples shared in common all that they owned, and it became clear to me at that moment how the House of Mercy had become a Christian community of the poor. What had begun as an inner city outreach to the poor had become something far more important. The House of Mercy had become a 'church of the poor'.

It was this communion of the poor which would save the House of Mercy in this dire time of need, when the limited resources of the staff were being stretched beyond the breaking point. When the staff was dropping balls, the poor and homeless guests were there to pick them up and the volunteer network swelled as the guests recognized the growing needs of their compatriots. It was clearly a witness to something greater than all of us. Blessed indeed are the poor, for to them has been given the power to usher in the Kingdom of God.

Caesar's Money

It felt wrong sitting there in the lobby of the Arc of Monroe County filling out an application for employment, and it wasn't just because of the pride I was swallowing. Here I was crawling back to my previous employer after only three short months at the House of Mercy. The real emotional struggle had to do with the feeling that I was somehow abandoning my post and selling out to manna—or at least my humble version of manna. I lived in a small two-bedroom house that I purchased a couple of years previously from the Department of Housing and Urban Development (HUD). It was in distressed condition and my partner Dave and I had spent the better part of the last two years living on a construction site. To cover the cost of purchasing and rehabbing the property, I had taken out a modest home equity loan and now I ran the risk of foreclosure and homelessness if I continued to work at the House of Mercy on a hope and a prayer, as I had been for the past two weeks. Nonetheless, as I sat in a padded wooden chair facing a pair of automatic sliding doors, whose usage was annoyingly frequent, I couldn't exorcise the feeling that I simply did not measure up to the level of dedication demonstrated by the other staff members at the House of Mercy.

Shaking off thoughts of my inadequacy, I returned to the task at hand, repositioning the clipboard in my lap and beginning the long litany of useless higher degrees under the "education" heading on the employment application form. I knew the position in which I would be placed would be something that anyone with a high school diploma could fill. When I had finished pointlessly listing my references that they would certainly never call, I sat there momentarily frozen in my shame and disappointment. Releasing the breath I had been anxiously holding, I rose to my feet and nonchalantly tossed the clipboard through the slot in the receptionist's window. She breezed over the application, frowning briefly in a moment of puzzlement as she glanced at the Ph.D. and other over-qualifications, and then informed me to sit back down.

"You're lucky. Today we're doing interviews on the spot," she said giving a halfhearted attempt at sounding bouncy and customer oriented. Here was the cumulative contribution of all of those Total Quality Management seminars that the employees had been compelled to attend at the Arc of Monroe—feigned buoyancy. She made a few checkmarks in the margins of my application form, unclipped it from the clipboard, then spun around in her office chair and stood up to rush out of her cubicle, all in a single motion.

I sat back in my hallway chair and drank in the nervous monotony of those jerky mechanical doors which were neurotically triggered by an electric eye any time someone walked within 15 feet of the entrance. I was unpleasantly unsurprised when the receptionist returned in a matter of minutes and informed me that the manager of one of the group homes wanted to interview me. I walked into a small back office where I was met by a white female in her mid-twenties with a BSW in one hand and a year and a half of experience working with the developmentally disabled in the other. She seemed to be possessed by some mysterious, apprehensive energy that was, at the same time, sapping her of her own essential life force. Her sunken eyes, disheveled hair, and universally jerky movements belied the confident professional facade that hovered just above the surface of her troubled waters. Obviously, she had just hit the big time by landing her first managerial position at a notorious residence for dually-diagnosed individuals with extreme behavior problems. Those who had hired her had undoubtedly told her that Brooks Avenue was a difficult place to manage, but that was why they were handing the task over to someone of her unique talents, i.e., she was the only one inexperienced and naïve enough to apply. She asked me the questions that she had been asked when she was hired: what would you do if...? How would you respond to...? When thus and so happens would you explain the correct procedure? In the end, I avoided any facetious or cynical answers. And so I was hired and my soul that day was sold at the bargain basement price of $18,000 per year.

That night, as I relayed the "good" news to Dave, I could see that he was reading my own disappointment in spite of the rosy analysis I was giving to the situation. His responses were measured and cautious as he entered the minefield of my ambivalent emotional landscape.

"Well, aahhh, you never know. This move might lead to something you really want to do…You know, you didn't have to take the job at the Arc. I'm making enough to pay for both of us."

"Yeah, yeah," I said, dismissively. "But that wouldn't be fair, making you carry the entire load while I pursue my interests. Anyway, you need to start saving for your retirement." Dave Campbell was a sixty-year-old man who had spent most of his life in Canada. We had met in Toronto while I was in my second year of coursework in the doctoral program. He was a powerfully built, stocky, balding man of Irish and Scottish decent with a Popeye voice that belied his singularly gentle and generous character. He was a talented industrial electrician who was cursed with an alcoholic chemistry. He had hospitalized himself on several occasions and one of his binges had landed him on the streets of Toronto for a number of years. At the time we met in a downtown bar, he had turned back to the bottle seeking comfort from the demon of loneliness. I discovered his affliction after we moved into an apartment together and I promptly made arrangements to leave. When I could not immediately find affordable accommodations on my teaching assistant's salary, I was forced to stay a little bit longer. He promised to quit drinking if I promised to stay longer, and now four years later both promises had yet to be broken.

Dave responded to my retirement suggestions by mumbling something unintelligible and casting his eyes downward as though he had just been chastised by an angry parent.

"Oh, I almost forgot!" I said, suddenly remembering a request C.W. had made last week. "C.W. was wondering if you could come over some night, at your convenience, and install the new permanent steel door in the basement. He's worried the one that's there isn't going to last much longer."

"Oh yeah. That's for sure," said Dave, awakening from his funk over the retirement issue. "He got those hollow interior doors from Mr. Second—I'm pretty sure of that. And those things won't hold up long against the kind of punishment they get over there."

"I told him I'd call him tonight. When do you think you can make it?" I queried.

"How about tonight?" Dave responded, surprising me with his willingness to go into action on a moment's notice.

"That would be great! I'll call C.W. to see if that'll work for him," I said, reaching for the phone.

C.W. was thrilled to hear that Dave could do the job so soon and promptly invited us to come over and install the door. Dave visited the House of Mercy once before when the new building was still under construction. He only met construction workers on that trip. This time he would meet the real House of Mercy crowd and I was concerned about how he would respond to an environment that most volunteers found unsettling at best. But Dave showed no signs of anxiety or hesitation so we packed up his tools and headed off in his van.

The ride from my house to the House of Mercy somehow always felt longer in a car than on a bicycle. Apparently the way one perceives time is altered by the degree of one's closeness to the pavement. In any case, the ride on that drizzly, dark night seemed longer than usual for whatever reason. We rode silently giving me an opportunity to rehearse the way I would introduce Dave to the staff and guests. Many already knew something about Dave and he certainly had gotten to know most of the characters at the House of Mercy through my daily updates that summer. Still, I was a little anxious regarding the relative success of this anticipated encounter between my two households.

We snaked our way through a good portion of the labyrinthine hallways at the House of Mercy before we ran into C.W., which was just as well because it became an opportunity to give a tour of the property.

"Hey, C.W." I said, as we came up behind him.

"Whoa, hey Tom...This is Dave I presume," he said, as he smiled warmly and reached out his hand to Dave.

"Yeah, hi C.W." Dave said shaking the hand that was offered.

"Can I get you anything to eat or drink before we get started?" C.W. generously proposed.

"No thanks, we just ate," I informed him.

C.W. escorted us to the basement and laid out the general plan for where he thought the door ought to be situated. After posing some technical questions, Dave suggested a few modifications to the plan which would lead to greater security and longevity for the door. I could see that C.W. was pleasantly impressed by Dave's expertise, and after about fifteen minutes, a detailed agreement had been struck regarding the way we would proceed. On two or three occasions during the whole process a guest or staff member came through in order to speak to C.W. about some issue of concern. Dave was introduced to each person and, although he met some of our toughest cases that evening, he never appeared unsettled or ruffled by the experience. I could see by the look on his face that C.W. was also taking note of Dave's admirable magnanimity.

Dave spent the next couple of hours framing and installing the door that would remain a major thoroughfare throughout the installation process. Every few minutes or so an individual, or caravan of workers, would need to pass, disrupting the work flow and often presenting new opportunities for introducing Dave to unfamiliar staff and guests. I labored as Dave's incompetent assistant, handing him tools, or carrying and holding things in place while he sawed, screwed and hammered his way ever closer to the finished product. Meanwhile, C.W. was uncharacteristically unoccupied and spent those hours chatting with Dave about various topics. They genuinely seemed to like one another in a natural sort of way, and by the end of the job, they had already made arrangements to work together on a few other undone maintenance projects around the House of Mercy over the next few weeks.

I was relieved and a little excited that Dave's introduction to the House of Mercy had gone so well that evening. As we all shook hands and bid farewell that night I could see by the friendly and warm expressions, and the lingering conversations, that the two households had forged an enduring bond. On the way home my enthusiasm bubbled over into verbosity regarding the many virtues of the House of Mercy and the numerous invaluable talents that Dave was bringing to the table. In the midst of all this needless rehashing and interpretation of the events of that night, I mentioned to Dave that he seemed much more at ease with the staff and guests at the House of Mercy than most first time volunteers. Without hesitation Dave broke silence and replied:

"I'm an alcoholic. I lived on the streets for years. I was alone and discarded by my family and friends. Everyone had given up on me. No one should be abandoned and alone."

This simple, succinct statement became a window into Dave's almost instant familiarity and solidarity with the people at the House of Mercy, and their reciprocal automatic embrace of Dave. Most well-meaning volunteers who came to this inner city outreach to the poor and homeless found themselves barraged by people and events which so overwhelmed their sense of personal well-being and security that they simply never returned. The unfed, the unwashed, the addicted, the violent, the mentally ill, the desperate and the exhausted all congregate inside those doors in a great mass of human need. Like Dave, all have been, in some dramatic way, alienated from the common social, economic and familial support structures which most of us take for granted. It also struck me that, like Dave, the staff at the House of Mercy also believed no one should be abandoned and alone. They both shared a theology of radical hospitality born from an intimate experience of being a stranger, a vulnerable person on the margins of society. They viewed hospitality as an end in itself—the ultimate test of our divine call to love our neighbor.

I knew, at that moment, this was a perspective I could share only by adoption. But that seemed to be the way that things were naturally ordered when viewed through the lens of a preferential option for the poor. Adoption, not heredity, was the sign of divine love. Sr. Grace and the other House of Mercy staff had adopted the poor and homeless and the homeless adopted the staff in return. Dave had adopted me and I in turn was adopting him and seeing with new eyes from his perspective. Like Ruth and Naomi, we love by adopting one another through this process of embracing as one's own, the otherness of another and relinquishing the exclusive ownership of our own otherness.

The following week I arrived early for our Forum meeting at Our Lady of Perpetual Help parish. Sr. Livia and I sat at the dining room table and exchanged small talk over a warm drink and cookies. Sr. Livia Ruocco was Sr. Gloria's sister as well as Sr. Grace and Fr. Neil's cousin. She worked as the Director of Faith Formation at OLPH and she was also a Sister of Mercy like her sister and cousin. She had taken the same courses that I taught at St. Bernard's Institute which Sr. Grace had taken one year ago. In that short time, those of us in the Forum had experienced so much together and had grown so close through dialogue that it seemed like we had known each other forever. I felt like I could share anything with almost anyone within the scope of the larger House of Mercy Family.

That evening Sr. Livia was sharing some of her struggles in her ministry at OLPH and I was figuratively crying on her shoulder about my decision to leave the House of Mercy and return to the security of social service employment. Fr. Neil was upstairs in his room at the rectory unwinding from a day of pastoring this eclectic parish family consisting of absentee suburbanites, a growing Hispanic minority and a nascent African American population fed, for the most part, by refugees from the weekly mass held at the House of Mercy. The weekly mass hadn't been going as well lately mainly because of a change in priestly leadership. The most recent celebrant and the congregation did not seem to be in synch with one another and many guests at the House of

Mercy had begun to complain about the style of the new celebrant. Sr. Grace had approached her brother about becoming the celebrant, but he was reluctant to step on anyone's toes, even if his intrusion would most likely have been welcome. Instead, he invited House of Mercy guests to his late morning Sunday liturgy at OLPH; however, they were quickly finding out that particular mass wasn't necessarily well suited to their needs either.

At the Forum the week before we briefly discussed the possibility of a gospel mass at OLPH. The discussion was tabled because we had more pressing concerns to discuss—most notably, Monroe County's commitment to an electronic finger imaging technology that was purportedly designed to reduce fraud among welfare recipients. We were suspicious of both the motive behind this implementation, and the efficacy of this draconian techno-surveillance of the poor. With the assistance of Sr. Grace and others in the Forum, I had conducted a thoroughgoing study of the technology and its pilot project implementation in two other New York Counties. I had been prepared to present my finding and lead a discussion on this issue. However, as Sr. Livia and I conversed at the dining room table I could hear the vanload of people from the House of Mercy coming in through the side door of OLPH's rectory and they seemed to have a burning issue of their own. As this rabble spilled into the hallways of the rectory, their hubbub put an end to the polite little mutual support group Sr. Livia and I had formed.

"Tom! Livia! Wait till you hear what happened to me today. You just won't believe it," said Sr. Grace as she greeted us with a hug and a kiss.

I could tell by the tone in her voice that her story was going to dominate our discussion that evening, so when I sat down I surreptitiously packed my notes back in my bag hoping that Grace would not see them and consequently censor her comments in deference to my prepared agenda. It had been my experience that this sort of spontaneous reflection on experience was often more productive than prepared "lectures."

Soon after the arrival of the House of Mercy contingent, Fr. Neil joined us from his second floor retreat, unable to resist the sounds of excitement coursing up the rectory stairs. When all the greetings had been accomplished—not an easy or nonchalant task—the banquet was prepared as food, drinks and deserts were arrayed before us forming a feast that seemed out of proportion to the number of people present. However, experience had taught that most of what was placed before this crowd would be miraculously consumed. As always, the atmosphere was festive and alive, unlike virtually any other social action planning meeting with which I had been associated. With everyone seated and after all the plates had been loaded to capacity, we were ready to begin, and quietly Sr. Gloria prompted me to start the meeting.

"I think it's time," she whispered with a doll's voice and a coy smile.

"OK. Well it seems my job is going to be easy tonight," I said, as everyone chuckled knowingly. "I think Sr. Grace had quite an eye opening experience today so without further delay I think we should hear about it."

"Thanks Tom," said Sr. Grace with a broad smile. "Most of you have already heard bits and pieces of the story of my day, but let me start at the beginning, which really takes us back a number of weeks when we had just moved into Hudson Avenue. At that time I was approached by Sr. Ann, our provincial for the Sisters of Mercy, and Sr. Sheila, our treasurer, who proposed that we designate the House of Mercy as a homeless shelter in order to attract state and local government funding. I explained to them that we had already explored that option and had rejected it because of the many restraints on our ministry that such a change of status would entail. I even listed some of the restraints for them. I also made the point that the House of Mercy was much more than a shelter and listed for them the things we do in addition to providing a place for people to sleep.."

"Like the clothing and the food," Tricky Dick added.

"Yeah, and all the counseling," Kevin piped in.

"Don't forget the Breakfast Club," said Greg.

All around the room each member of the Forum added to the litany as if we were all participating in a sermon by a tent revival preacher.

"That's right," Grace continued. "And I'm afraid that if we become a designated homeless shelter, so much of our energy would be spent satisfying and complying with various state and local regulations that we would essentially have to abandon our identity as a full service outreach—and that just wouldn't be acceptable."

"What was their reaction?" I asked. Grace continued.

"They were dismissive, saying that they thought I was exaggerating about the intrusiveness of the regulations and that the Sisters of Mercy needed the income from these various funding sources in order to pay the bills on the new building."

"Well, *do* they need that much money?" Fr. Neil asked.

"I don't really know," Grace answered. "They haven't let me see the financial statements on the new building. But we have always scraped by in the past by the grace of God and the generosity of our benefactors. I don't see why we would strike out after other sources of funding when we haven't given our traditional sources a chance to come through for us."

"The mother house has been trying to bring us under their thumb for years now," Sr. Rita commented. Grace concurred.

"And I think that's exactly what's going on here; but now they've stepped up their efforts and a conspiracy has developed among those in the most powerful positions at the mother house. This conspiracy is designed to oust the present staff so they can appoint people of their choosing, who see things their way. And if they had things their way, the House of Mercy would look exactly like every other homeless shelter in the city. The House of Mercy would then become a source of revenue for the order and would make them look good in the eyes of the powerful and wealthy. As it stands, they see us as an embarrassing drain of resources."

"So what happened today that was so special?" Fr. Neil asked.

"OK. Well…I'm getting to that," said Sr. Grace, tripping over her words to recompose her thoughts. "Anyway. At this meeting a few weeks ago, Ann invited me to a meeting she had arranged with a number of community leaders and government administrators under the guise of exploring funding options for the House of Mercy. That was the meeting I attended today."

"You use the word 'guise,' Grace, who was at this meeting and what was it about?" Asked Sr. Livia.

"Well, first of all, when I showed up I found out it wasn't just Ann and myself, but also Sheila and Sr. Pat, our new Associate Provincial, who oversees the various ministries conducted by the Sisters of Mercy."

"What were *they* doing there?" Sr. Gloria said, sounding surprised.

"I had no idea!" Grace continued. "I had the same question when we met outside before the meeting. Ann's explanation was that they were there to 'support' us. In truth, the three of them were there to drown out my voice and to speak authoritatively for the House of Mercy. I think they thought they could intimidate me or drown me out, and that's precisely how the meeting began. After being introduced as the director of the ministry, I wasn't consulted or even given a chance to speak by my fellow sisters. It took one of the government administrators, who addressed me specifically, to bring me into the discussion."

"Then what was the real purpose of the meeting?" I asked.

"Well. Get this!" Grace said excitedly. "After about twenty minutes of a presentation by the other three sisters it became clear to me they were proposing that the House of Mercy would become a shelter and that the city should provide the necessary funds to upgrade the building. At this point I jumped in saying that the House of Mercy didn't want to make the kinds of changes that were being proposed for both the ministry and the building. And I told them stories about the ministry and the people so they could get an idea of why we are so essential—just the way we are. At that point, an African American woman, who heads the city office in charge of administering HUD money, mentioned matter-of-factly that we couldn't receive funding from her office if we didn't make at least some of the changes the other sisters were proposing. So I said, 'we don't want your money. We just want to continue the work we have been doing.' At that point Ann jabbed me in the ribs with her elbow and when I turned, she looked at me with this wild-eyed, stern look and whispered in a voice loud enough for everyone to hear: 'Grace, we want Caesar's money!'"

A gasp of shock arose around the Forum from those who understood this baldly cynical biblical reference. Those who didn't understand the allusion looked around at the rest of us, searching for an explanation. Grace immediately recognized that the quote would require explanation for some of those present so she continued with an exegesis.

"Ann was referring to a Bible verse when she spoke of 'Caesar's money.' In that story those who were conspiring to destroy his movement approached Jesus late in his ministry. They asked him a question to trick him into saying something that would either get him arrested, or ruin his credibility with his followers. They asked him if the Jews should pay taxes to the Roman government. If he said, 'no,' they could have him arrested for insurrection. If he said, 'yes,' many of his followers would be scandalized by his betrayal of his Jewish identity. Paying taxes to Rome, for many Jews of this time, was equivalent to collaborating with the enemy. Instead of answering with a 'yes' or 'no' Jesus asked to see one of the coins used to pay the taxes. He asked his challengers 'whose image is on this coin?' They answered, 'Caesar's.' And Jesus replied, 'then render unto Caesar that which is Caesar's, and to God that which is God's'"

"So let me get this straight," Prince interjected, in his usual animated way, pausing strategically for dramatic effect. "Sr. Ann…your superior…said…in front of everybody…dat she wanted to collaborate with the enemy…as long as it was good for her?"

"That is exactly it Prince!" Grace exclaimed emphatically with a sense of satisfaction that her explanation had hit its mark. "I couldn't have said it better myself."

"That is so cynical," said Sr. Rita, shaking her head in disbelief. "I can't believe…no wait…I can believe she would say something that horrible. So what happened after she said that we wanted Caesar's money?"

"Well, for a moment I just stared at Ann in shock. I was waiting for her to laugh or something…say she was just kidding maybe," Grace explained. "When it was clear she was serious, I turned to look at the others seated around the table. I saw various expressions ranging from disbelief to disgust. I was mortified to be associated with her. I thought I would never say this, but at that moment I was ashamed to be a Sister of Mercy."

"Yeah, well I'm feeling a little ashamed myself just hearing you tell the story," said Rita, with a hint of anger in her voice.

As I had foreseen earlier in the evening, the Forum's discussion was dominated by this issue for the remainder of the night. Ultimately, desire for 'Caesar's money' would become a shorthand way of referring to any kind of betrayal at the House of Mercy. What was at stake was far more than simply the acceptance or rejection of a certain stream of funding. In fact, the House of Mercy had received government funds in the past and would continue to do so into the future. The question was under whose terms those funds were accepted and whether or not that funding stream would require that we behave in such a way that would jeopardize our core beliefs and values. Apparently, for Ann and the other two sisters from the motherhouse, these were moot points. They wanted a lucrative funding stream and they were willing to betray the House of Mercy's essential character to ensure the receipt of those funds. Fundamental questions of identity and purpose were posed to all of us that evening. Whose face would the House of Mercy wear? To whom would we belong? How would we remain faithful to the families we have adopted if we have made alliances with powers that would erase rather than embrace their otherness?

The answers uniting those of us around the table that evening would, at the same time, divide the Sisters of Mercy in Rochester in the years to come. From that day forward, relations between the House of Mercy and the motherhouse progressively deteriorated. At the center of the division was the issue of identity. Fundamental to the House of Mercy's identity was an unfailing commitment to those poor and marginalized family members whom we had chosen and who had, in turn, chosen us. Others seemed to believe the House of Mercy should become some kind of pipeline tapped directly into the vaults of Caesar's money.

Reality Cup

I composed the layout and the carefully worded text of our "Reality Cup" flyer in my head on my twenty-minute drive from my new place of work in Webster, NY. The Forum had broadened its membership earlier in the summer of 1995, morphing into a larger coalition known as the Metropolitan Forum, which included a number of other neighborhood organizations and grass roots associations from across the city. I had relinquished my leadership role around the same time in order to focus my energies on the ministry position I had accepted at Holy Trinity Parish, which was located in a northeastern suburb of Rochester. I had resisted entering ministry for the past few years because I was convinced that ministry required a degree of commitment that I could not offer. I had been focused on finding a job teaching at a university during this period; however, my endurance was beginning to fail in the face of unrelenting rejection. Therefore, I finally decided that it was no longer dishonest for me to seek a more productive outlet for my Ph.D. than those which could be found in direct care services for the developmentally disabled. So late in the Spring of 1995 I gave up the search for academic employment, as well as my job at Brooks Avenue Group Home, and threw myself into full time ministry as a Director of Faith Formation.

The Reality Cup was the premier brainchild of the newly organized Metropolitan Forum, which was finding new ideas and energy from Dr. John Klofas, a professor of criminology at the Rochester Institute of Technology. He had originally come into contact with the House of Mercy this past Winter when he volunteered to assist in a fund raising campaign organized by the Sisters of Mercy. When he found out about our history of protest and direct action for justice he was immediately drawn to what we were doing in the Forum since he had been advocating for many of the same causes. John was a big man with an even bigger presence who was intelligent, energetic, and had many important contacts in the community. His solid frame and reddish beard gave him a Grizzly Adams appearance. Although he came with many ideas and an agenda of his own, he had a generous and flexible spirit that allowed him to be open to hearing other points of view.

It was John's idea to use the Ryder Cup golf tournament, which was being held that summer at the Country Club of Rochester, for a consciousness raising campaign aimed at drawing attention to the plight of the poor in the inner city. Because the Ryder Cup would be the highlight of the professional golf season that summer, it had the potential of attracting international attention to the embarrassing degree of poverty that existed in parts of that city. Because golf was a game traditionally played by wealthy and elite classes, the event, its participants and its milieu would serve as a striking contrast to the homeless protesters from the House of Mercy. Naming our series of actions, "Reality Cup," which was Sr. Grace's idea, served to shed light, not simply on the harsh realities of the poorest neighborhoods, but also on the pretentious, illusory and fantastic character of the Ryder Cup.

The task of composing and laying out the flyer had fallen to me due to the fact that I was the only one in the Metropolitan Forum who had the equipment and requisite technical skill. It was a role I seemed to play no matter with whom or what I became involved. Already at my new job at Holy Trinity I was identified as the person who was going to computerize the office and network all of the computers so they could "talk" to one another. This predicament was largely of my own making since I had shamelessly promoted my computer skills during the interview process hoping that would improve my chances of being hired. These little technical tidbits might have increased my chances of being hired, but they also definitely increased my eventual workload, which would soon amount to sixty and seventy hour weeks when the school year began.

My bike bumped and rattled around in the back of my little Subaru wagon as I negotiated the cracked and pockmarked pavement traveling along at a healthy clip. I had taken my bike to work at the request of my new boss, Fr. Tom Nellis, because he wanted to mix business with pleasure that afternoon. The plan was to bring me up to date concerning the immediate issues and needs in the parish, while, of course, enjoying a relaxing ride along country roads. The business part of the afternoon was not neglected; however, the bicycle trip was cut short when Fr. Nellis suffered a flat tire only a few miles into the ride. Abandoning the bikes by the side of the road, we sat underneath a tree for most of that sunny afternoon and laid the groundwork for what would become for me a most rewarding friendship, as well as an invaluable professional experience.

On my way home I passed Mid-Town Tennis Club, which I had recently joined. On the day I joined I was promptly recruited by the Head Tennis Pro Willie Schutte to help with the junior development program. I was a mediocre player, but so were most of the juniors so I was in good company. On court, my role with the juniors had less to do with tennis and more to do with conditioning and speed work. In exchange for my services, I received a free membership and was given the opportunity to drill with the advanced juniors in the late afternoon. I loved playing tennis and the exercise was a real stress buster, but the Mid-Town context was about as far removed from my experiences at the House of Mercy as one could possibly imagine.

Mid-Town marketed itself as a fitness destination for rich and influential Rochesterians. It was an indoor version of a rather exclusive country club where CEO's would congregate to network and be noticed by their peers. There were also lesser folk represented among the membership, but no one very far down the rungs on the social and economic ladder. Then there was me, who just wanted to play tennis and innocently blundered into this place thinking I would probably be able to swing the membership fee on my new bloated salary of $25,000 per year. I guffawed loudly when the "Membership Associate" blithely quoted me the yearly rate. Overhearing my reaction, Willie Schutte offered to take me out on the court to hit some balls. In the course of half an hour of hitting and chatting we had worked out the arrangement noted above.

I could see the series of rectangular concrete and steel buildings that made up the Mid-Town complex pass beneath me as I drove along the exchange ramp that connected interstate I/590 south to I/490 west. I chuckled as my gaze fixed momentarily on those imposing monuments to wealth. It occurred to me that tonight's meeting of the Metropolitan Forum would be sort of a personal version of a "Reality Cup" for me. My life was quickly becoming dominated by a job in a suburb interspersed with recreation among the rich and infamous at an exclusive tennis club. The contrast between the country club fantasia of the Rochester Ryder Cup and the harsh realities of the poorest neighborhoods was striking and ironically parallel to the contrast between the nascent realities in my own life and the House of Mercy.

I would have no time for tennis this evening since I had to get home, eat dinner, and put this flyer together all in the space of a little more than an hour and a half. Tonight's meeting would be held in the same House of Mercy conference room where Sr. Gloria held her tutoring sessions with school age children. This was supposed to be our last meeting on the Reality Cup before launching into our various direct action campaigns. Beyond my editorial duties in regards to the brochure, I was scheduled to be a picketer at the Country Club of Rochester on two of the afternoons during the golf tournament. Other activities included letters to the editors, media conferences, a poor people's miniature golf tournament catered by one of the area soup kitchens, and a commemorative Reality Cup mug and baseball cap—all of which, in a paradoxically modest way, mirrored trappings of the far more elaborate Ryder Cup.

I drafted the brochure that evening as a gobbled down dinner and casually scanned the news on television. After cleaning the dishes, I dashed upstairs and relentlessly typed the text into a template which automatically placed things precisely where they were supposed to go, saving me time, effort and considerable stress. Snatching the brochure out of the printer as the final characters were being formed, I careened down the stairs, out the front door, and drove away in a mad rush only to arrive at the meeting a good ten minutes before anyone else. I had neglected once again to factor in CP time.

Greetings and pleasantries were exchanged as one-by-one the Forum members gathered around the table that only a year ago I had stripped, sanded and finished as the House of Mercy moved from Central Park to Hudson Avenue. Just as C.W. predicted, over the course of just a few months the pristine Hudson Avenue location had been transformed into a far more funky version of its renovated self. This second "renovation" occurred gradually as the people settled in and made the place their own. Now there was no mistaking 725 Hudson Avenue for anything other than the House of Mercy. Sr. Grace no longer worried about whether the people would feel at home, since that concern had been answered long ago. As I examined the conference table top I noticed each of the scratches, chips and coffee mug stains that had accumulated during the course of the year. Already that table told a story and I was proud to have been the one who laid the polyurethane foundation for each sentence in that saga.

The Metropolitan Forum was far more business-like than the Rochester People's Forum could ever have hoped to be. Like our other meetings under the able leadership of John Klofas, this one had an agenda with time limits, and the proceedings were conducted under the rubrics of Robert's Rules in which we always brought resolutions to a vote and took minutes that would be faithfully read at the subsequent meeting. While some of us longed for the free-form, disordered bull sessions of our former incarnation, there were some of us who found the new rigor refreshing and invigorating. One apparent dissenter was Tricky Dick whom I had not seen for a number of months. I had been meaning to inquire concerning his whereabouts for a few weeks, but it always seemed to slip my mind. Tonight I was determined to be more disciplined so during our ten minute break I approached Grace, C.W. and Rita, who were eating cookies and soda and sharing some semi-confidential information since they were huddled together speaking in hushed voices.

"Howdy. Mind if I join in?" I said.

"Oh, hi Tom," said Grace, smiling and shifting her gaze around making eye contact with those gathered in order to determine if the topic being discussed should be shared. "We were just having a conversation about one of the people. The information is confidential."

"Oh, sorry. I understand. I was just wondering how Tricky Dick was doing," I said, preparing to dismiss myself from a conversation apparently not meant for my ears.

The others in the small confidentiality cadre laughed in unison. Rita then exclaimed,

"That's who we were just talking about!" Grace then interjected, speaking to the whole group she said,

"Tom knows Tricky Dick well enough, and he was on staff so we know he can be faithful to our need for confidentiality, so why don't we just bring him up to speed? C.W., you're the best informed about Tricky's situation; can you give a summary of what's been happening?"

"Yeah," C.W. began. "Well Tom, you know Trick well enough to know he had an addiction problem for most of his adult life. Well, guess what?" He asked rhetorically, shrugging his shoulders and gesturing palms up.

"He's back to his old ways," I said, answering his rhetorical question.

C.W. clapped his hands lightly and pointed in my direction saying,

"Give the man a cigar."

"He comes into my office high every day and, Tom, you've never seen Trick when he's high, but he's a completely different person," said Rita, as others seconded her opinion of Tricky Dick's transformation while under the influence. "You know him as a gentle, soft-spoken Teddy Bear of a guy, but when he's drunk or on crack he's mean, aggressive and every other word out of his mouth is some sort of curse. He's just been incorrigible the past few weeks."

"He picked a fight with Prince today and got Prince all upset...so much so that he couldn't make it to this meeting tonight," Sr. Grace added.

C.W. summarized the dilemma for the staff: "We're not really sure what to do. We've all dealt with these problems before—even on a daily basis—but when it's someone you've grown to know, love and care about over the course of such a long period of time...well...it's just disappointing and heartbreaking—on top of being annoying and difficult."

I concurred, expressing my surprise and sadness at Tricky Dick's deteriorating condition. I asked if there was anything more we could do for Trick and received a unanimous request for prayers on his behalf.

Our little conspiracy was then broken up by John Klofas calling us back to order.

"Alright everybody, break's over. Let's get back to the business at hand so we can all get back home."

Speak for yourself John. I am home," C.W. quipped, referring to the fact that "home" for C.W. was a one-room apartment directly above the conference room where we were all gathered. We all laughed. John continued:

"Let's hear from Tom. Have you made any progress on our brochure since our last meeting?"

"Yup, and here's our draft, which is awaiting the Forum's approval." I said, passing copies of the brochure around the room. I proceeded to read it aloud so that even those who couldn't read could have input on its content.

"The Ryder Cup is a chance to showcase our community to the world. We are all proud to attract such a prestigious event and to show the world our business, social and cultural accomplishments. But our community is not just a community of Fortune 500's, country clubs and the symphony. We live in a diverse community in which many people are struggling. For a full sense of our community, we should also showcase that struggle.

WELCOME TO THE REALITY CUP. WELCOME TO...

• Monroe County—where over 100,000 households are low-income households (U.S. Census Bureau)

• Monroe County—where two-thirds of city residents and one-third of suburban residents live in low-income households (U.S. Census Bureau)

• Monroe County—where more than one of every 20 residents receives welfare (State of Greater Rochester 1993)

• Monroe County—where the official Child Health Report Card shows that the County is the home to increasing poverty, infant mortality, teenage pregnancy, and violence (Pathways, University of Rochester and Monroe County Department of Health)

• Monroe County—which ranks worst in the nation in affordable rental housing and among the worst in the number of substandard rental units (Center on Budget and Policy Priorities)
• Monroe County—where 30,700 manufacturing jobs have been lost since 1981 (Pathways)

• Rochester—where black unemployment is higher today than it was at the time of the riots 30 years ago (U.S. Census Bureau)

• Rochester—which is first among major cities in branch bank location disparity and where national media has recognized discriminatory practices in home mortgage lending (U.S. News and World Report; Greater Rochester Community Reinvestment Coalition)

• Rochester—where over one half of all

neighborhoods are classified as poor, and the poverty rate is four times the rate of the suburbs (U.S. Census Bureau)

• Rochester—where 80% of public school children are eligible for the free lunch program, and the city ranks 13th in the nation in child mortality—higher than New York City (Pathways)

• Rochester—where fewer students receive Regents diplomas today than seven years ago and which leads the state in dropout and suspension rates (N.Y.S. Education Department; Democrat and Chronicle)

• Rochester—where the homicide rate for young black males in poverty is equal to wartime casualty rates (Metropolitan Forum)

Welcome to Monroe County, the home of the Ryder Cup and the city which is on the brink of the point of no return. (David Rusk)"

When I finished reading I instinctively picked up a pen in preparation for the inevitable revisions, but no one seemed anxious to edit or amend the script which would ultimately become our official propaganda for our various actions during the coming weeks. In fact, the brochure received universal and unmitigated praise and I spent the drive home pondering the secret to its success. Never had so spontaneous an effort on my part produced such a singularly untarnished result. However, the Forum represented a very selective group of readers and listeners for this kind of literature. As a pulled in my narrow driveway I wondered how those gathered for the Ryder Cup spectacle would receive our message.

"Go fuck yourself and your goddamn Reality Cup you humorless bastards!" A man in his mid-forties profaned from the driver's seat of his late model Mercedes-Benz as he tore up our brochure, spit on it, and tossed it out his tinted window. The car then sped away down the long driveway leading onto the property of the Country Club of Rochester. Yesterday afternoon we had been thrown off the premises right under the noses of both local and national media. Today we were permitted to come no closer than the gate, where we held placards, chanted slogans, and handed out brochures. Unfortunately, our depiction on the evening news had been less than sympathetic. The personnel who were sent by the TV, radio and newspapers to these sorts of events apparently lacked a sensitivity for social justice and activism. Sound bites from the country club owner, interspersed with scenes of angry protesters, made us appear crazed and unbalanced, and possibly even a little bit comical—none of which had been in our original plan for media coverage of the Reality Cup.

Nonetheless, our Reality Cup miniature golf tournament held the previous weekend had been a hit with both the homeless and the media who came out to cover the event. Our depiction in the media was very positive. John Klofas and Sr. Grace were given ample time for soundbites, while the tournament images portrayed the Forum as fun and creative in addition to the obvious social message in contrast to the Ryder Cup. In the days that followed, Sr. Grace received numerous unexpected calls from the powerful and well-heeled members of the community expressing their support and pledging significant donations.

This was the last day of the Ryder Cup and, therefore, our last day of direct action in relation to this event. The hats and coffee cups had sold well bringing in a few hundred dollars for the House of Mercy. Generally speaking, most of us had enjoyed our part in the various events, though we were also looking forward to a well-deserved break from the intensity of the preparations and execution of Reality Cup. By late afternoon the traffic had dwindled to a trickle and we were consulting one another about packing up Reality Cup and heading back to the House of Mercy for the post-event party. Just then a late model Cadillac slowly pulled up beside me and the rear passenger-side window came down with a whine to reveal the concerned face of an elderly woman who said to me:

"Do you need a ride dear?"

"Excuse me?" I responded pointing at my chest. "Are you speaking to me?"

"Yes. I imagined your car had broken down." She said, pointing to an oddly parked BMW at the curb nearby.

"Oh no, that's not mine." I responded, puzzled by this line of inquiry.

"Well, in any case, your kind will fare better if you stay among your own." She said with a familiar wink, solicitously gesturing me to join her in the back seat. I retorted politely, though a little indignantly, "I am with *my own*, right where I am, thank you." And with that she turned away and raised her whiny window as the driver slowly pulled away. For a moment I stood frozen by the incongruity of the last exchange. I examined myself for any evidence that might have suggested to her that I belonged among those who were behind the gates of the Country Club of Rochester. My assumed innocence was soon shattered, for sure enough, I was dressed head to toe in my tennis duds, which I had not bothered to change out of as I rushed to our final Reality Cup action. There I stood like an illusory island of superficial privilege, juxtaposed against the more genuinely mundane backdrop of my fellow protesters who were thankfully oblivious to the recent incident of mistaken identity. Possibly more than anyone else in Rochester that day, I needed a cup full of reality.

That night I felt compelled, for some reason, to pick up the guitar that I only played occasionally since my hey days at Crittenden Day Treatment Center, and began strumming and plucking familiar tunes. After playing myself into a state of mild boredom, I picked up one of my songbooks to see if I could find something more interesting. The first song I opened to was the Shaker Hymn, which had been one of the three pieces I performed for my audition to music school (a brief, one semester fling at Ithaca College before heading to the seminary). I didn't need the music because I still knew it by heart. As I sang those words I couldn't help thinking about Tricky Dick, the Reality Cup and my own situation that was taking me further and further from the House of Mercy. In varying and unique ways it seemed to speak to all three equally well.

> Tis' a gift to be simple
> Tis' a gift to be free
> Tis' a gift to come down
> Where we ought to be
> And when we find ourselves
> in that place just right
> Twill be in the valley
> of love and delight.
>
> When true simplicity is gained
> To bow and to bend shant be afraid
> To turn, turn, will be our delight
> Till by turning, turning we come round right.

Idols of Security

I sat ruminating in the basement office at Holy Trinity Church that I shared with the bookkeeper and the parish photocopy machine—which attracted more than its share of sundry characters in need of its reproductive capacity. This morning had been unusually disruptive due to the breakdown of the photocopy machine over at the Holy Trinity grade school next door. A lull in the action had opened a window of opportunity for Pam Schultz, the bookkeeper, and I to get some work done. I was preparing my lesson plan for the RCIA session that week and Pam was busy performing some mysterious bookkeeper's voodoo on the computer over in her corner of the basement. Pam was a marvel, seemingly incapable of rancor or moodiness, and perpetually good humored and generous. We had become friends almost instantly upon my arrival a couple of years ago and we spent a good portion of our days easily solving personal, parish, community, city, national and international problems. She and her family, who shared an equivalent good cheer, lived a short mile away in a beautiful home built by her husband. But the Pamela charm felt oddly disordered this morning and it wasn't just because we had been invaded by teachers and staff from the grade school. We had been through far worse without witnessing so much as a ripple in her generally tranquil psychic pools. I had an uneasy feeling something more fundamental was bothering Pam, so I began to probe:

"Pam? Are you feeling all right? You seem a little down."

Pam paused, and then let out a deep breath.

"Is it that obvious?" She asked. "I've been trying to keep a stiff upper lip, but I guess I'm not a very good actress." She delivered the last few words followed by a fatalistic laugh. Although she was smiling, the stress she was under was visible through the mirthful façade.

"We're buds Pam," I reminded her. "Tell me about it."

"Well..." She started tentatively, clearly not sure whether she wanted to tell me. "You have to promise not to mention this to anyone else. Denny [Pam's husband] swore me to secrecy."

"I wouldn't tell anyone something you had told me in confidence," I said reassuringly.

"I know you wouldn't," Pam said in an affectionate tone. "Denny and I just want to keep this under wraps until we decide what we're going to do."

"What kind of trouble are you in?" I asked.

"Well, you know how I came on full time last month and all. Well, that wasn't really because I wanted more work here at the parish. Denny and I are having financial trouble and we need my paltry income to make ends meet these days. The building trades are in a slump lately. Denny is an honest bidder on his jobs. He never low-balls buyers in the bidding stage only to slap them with a huge bill at the closing. Most other builders have gotten into that practice and it's eating away at Denny's established markets. It has gotten so bad that we're afraid we might have to give up the house." Pam delivered the last few words with increasing emotion. I wasn't sure what to say, so I just gave her a hug and patted her on the back. Pam continued as we released our embrace.

"We've worked hard all of our lives, Tom. We haven't squandered what we've earned on high living and we have sacrificed a lot for our family, our Church and our community. I've taken all of this to prayer, but I just don't understand how God is working in this situation. We're so frustrated. We're really at wits end."

As Pam continued to describe her circumstances, it occurred to me that I had heard a strikingly similar story of suburban working class woe only a week ago from a couple in Holy Trinity's RCIA program. Since Pam knew the couple well and they had not seemed concerned about maintaining confidentiality regarding their situation, I decided to share their story with Pam.

"Pam, you know Brenda and Duane Chevalier don't you?" I asked.

"Yeah, of course. Brenda and I go way back. How are they doing in the RCIA?" Pam responded, shifting out of her sullen mood. I continued:

"Well, they're doing fine in the RCIA. In fact, some nights they are the ones who really make the entire process work. They know how to ask just the right questions at just the right times. However, after our latest RCIA meeting they relayed a very similar story to yours of financial struggle. In case you didn't know, Duane works for the County, driving trucks in the summer and snowplows in the winter. It seems that this winter has been so warm and dry that Duane has had no overtime at all. Apparently, they rely on overtime pay during the winter season to maintain their rather modest lifestyle. Brenda is afraid she will be forced to go to work even though she had planned to delay entering the workforce until her two year old daughter, Andrea, entered the first grade.."

"That's just a shame," said Pam, genuinely concerned for her friends. "You know Tom, most people assume because a person lives in a nice suburb, then that person must be well off and financially secure. But, in reality, only a few contracts, or a few paychecks separate us from the homeless people at the House of Mercy where you work. We aren't so different as we're led to believe."

I was struck by Pam's spontaneous and immediate grasp of the rather abstract notion of solidarity found in the venerable principles of Catholic social thought. Her understanding of the fraternal and spiritual bond, not only between herself and other working class families, but also between people of different economic classes, was born from her experience of personal financial struggle. That experience, in turn, exposed the fragile and thin layer of security which served as a barrier between the faux middle-class lifestyle of the American working class and the far harsher realities of poverty.

Just then my phone rang. Excusing myself from our conversation, I spun around in my office chair and picked up the receiver, delivering my canned professional greeting.

"Good morning, Holy Trinity Parish, Tom O'Brien speaking."

"Hi Tom, it's Grace. How ya doin'?" Sister Grace asked.

"Oh, hey, I'm fine," I responded. "This is such a coincidence. Pam and I were just talking about the House of Mercy."

"You were?" Grace exclaimed. "Well maybe that's why my ears are ringing."

"What are you doing calling at this time of the day?" I asked, genuinely surprised by Grace's call at this relatively early hour of the day.

"Tom, you know the struggle we've been having with the Department of Social Services and the City over our policy never to turn anyone away, and to allow guests to sleep overnight on the sofas and chairs even though we are not legally designated as a shelter," Grace said. After my acknowledgement she continued. "Well, that whole issue is coming to a showdown really soon. The City code inspectors came through a week ago and cited us for violations of the zoned use of our facility, which they claim is not equipped to handle overnight sleeping arrangements. Also, the Director of the local DSS, Richard Schauseil, has gotten the Mayor involved and just yesterday I had a long talk on the phone with the Mayor about our mission. He told me he is personally going to investigate this issue and bring it to some sort of resolution. He seemed angry, but fair."

"Well that seems hopeful," I interjected.

"Tom, I'm afraid we are facing a number of powerful foes in this battle, who are determined to pit the Mayor against us. We angered a lot of people in local government this fall, especially in the DSS, when we held our protest at their offices in September. They are the ones behind this current campaign to have us shut down. I can't rely on support from the Sisters of Mercy because they basically agree with the reasoning of those who want to see us closed, or turned into a traditional shelter. To make things worse, just two days ago I had a heated discussion on the phone with the DSS director and he ended up threatening us with a lawsuit for our protest against fingerimaging, saying that he was going to charge us with criminal trespass with the intent to obstruct a necessary service. Can you believe that?! He's accusing the House of Mercy of acting as an obstacle to their services when we have probably brought more people to them over the years than any other single organization in the City!"

"You said the Mayor was angry, but fair. What was the 'fair' part of your conversation with him?" I asked. Grace replied.

"He said he was going to spend the next month investigating the accusations against us as well as scrutinizing our claims that we are the only agency in town that will accept anyone and everyone regardless of circumstances or condition. At the end of this investigation he indicated that he would decide whether or not the City would continue to support the House of Mercy ministry within its borders."

"So our fate depends, to some extent, on who he talks to and what spin he receives," I said, drawing a hermeneutical conclusion.

"I'm worried," Grace said after a moment of silence. "I think it's time for the community to have input into this process. I want to hold a rally at the House of Mercy the night before the Mayor is scheduled to make his announcement. Let *him* see…let *us* see, the kind of support that exists out there on the street for the things we do. If the support isn't there, then we have no business leaving our doors open. But if we do have popular support, they'll have to drag us away by force."

"I'm behind you one hundred percent," I declared. "What is the date and time, and what do you want me to do?"

"The rally will be at 6:00pm on January 15th," Grace answered. "We'll talk about what we are going to do at the rally at our Forum meeting next week. Can you make it?"

"I'm pretty sure I can. My schedule is surprisingly flexible this Advent so you can count me in," I replied.

"That's great," Grace continued. "We'll contact you when we have a date and time."

The Forum had been working on the issue of the proposed fingerimaging of welfare recipients for almost three years. A few months before, in the fall of 1996, these systems had finally been installed at the Monroe County Department of Social Services, which also happened to be where many of the guests at the House of Mercy went to receive their benefits. Intense preparation went into our protests at the County Legislature, including data gathering, library research, interviews and numerous road trips to other New York State County Departments of Social Service where these same fingerimaging systems had been implemented as pilot projects. The fruit of our labor was a body of evidence that constituted a thorough indictment against these expensive surveillance techniques that were designed to humiliate and discourage the poor, while placating the wealthy and middle class with comforting illusions regarding the security of their hard earned tax dollars.

We began our deliberations on the data we had gathered about welfare fingerimaging by observing that recipients of public assistance have been traditionally viewed with suspicion and contempt by much of the rest of the population. This attitude was especially prevalent among those who constituted the upper and middle classes, and those who were their so-called representatives in government. Especially during the decade of the 1990's, these elite sectors and their many allies among the middle class successfully pushed volumes of regulations designed to keep track of every last penny spent by welfare recipients. These intrusive surveillance techniques made certain that those who received benefits were destitute and would remain so into the foreseeable future. To receive benefits one could possess virtually no savings, no income and no property of any value.

It was our suspicion that the "welfare reform," of the mid-1990's, which proposed to "do away with welfare as we know it," was being designed in relation to the institutional need to keep governmental expenditures at a minimum as more and more Americans found themselves among the underclass. In the process of lowering costs, these "reforms" would inevitably, reduce benefits, restrict access to benefits, build more and greater obstacles into the application process, force recipients to work at jobs paying well below the minimum wage, and increase control and surveillance techniques to barely tolerable levels.

Among the numerous "reforms" to public assistance under experimentation in New York State was this new fingerimaging technology, which claimed to reduce welfare fraud by ensuring a recipient would receive benefits only once. Under the proposed fingerimaging reform, recipients of welfare would be required, as a condition for receiving benefits, to place both index fingers on a computer camera that would record and store every swirl and ridge. A facial photograph would then be taken as well. In subsequent processing the recipient would repeat laying their fingers on the camera so that caseworkers could call up records and facial photographs on the screen. The computer would also scan its fingerprint file to determine whether the recipient was registered under another name.

The fingerimaging system claimed to significantly reduce welfare fraud by precluding anyone from receiving benefits more than once, a practice often referred to as "double dipping." However, it had not been demonstrated that "double dipping" constituted anything more than a tiny percentage of welfare fraud. The primary type of fraud in the welfare system involved working at an unreported job and drawing welfare payments at the same time. Fraud—of all kinds—accounted for 1-2% of the total cost of the welfare system according to the director of quality assurance and audit for the New York State DSS.

Those who were promoting fingerimaging for public assistance denied that there was any criminal stigma associated with fingerprinting. Many supporters would refer to having been fingerprinted themselves for one kind of public service or another. However, the involuntary nature of welfare fingerprinting by contrast to the voluntary nature of public service fingerprinting precluded, from the perspective of the Forum, any facile analogies. Most people associated involuntary forms of fingerprinting with the criminal justice system. With the institution of fingerimaging technologies the DSS was contributing to the stigmatization of the poor. In popular wealthy and middle-class consciousness, the poor already were stereotyped as lazy, stupid, parasitical, and dishonest. From our point of view, fingerimaging technologies augmented and emphasized this already damaging identity by associating poverty with criminality.

An important question we asked in regards to the welfare system and fraud was: what groups are responsible for the greatest number of tax dollars lost? The establishment focused its investigations on the poor because they had already defined the poor as dishonest and cunning. However, many cases of welfare fraud were perpetrated by the bureaucrats who oversaw the distribution of benefits. In one such case, welfare workers in New York City charged welfare applicants anywhere from $750 to $1,500 to open false case claims. The fee varied depending on whether the applicants furnished their own forged documents. In cases like these, the poor were being bribed into fraud by the bureaucrats and then were penalized for taking the bribe.

In a 1996 report, The New York State Department of Social Services estimated that 3% of welfare clients received benefits to which they were not entitled. A significant percentage of this 3% was due to DSS staff errors, or unintentional mistakes by the client. There was no evidence that a significant number of individuals were using alternate identities to obtain additional benefits. Fingerimaging could only detect those trying to receive benefits under an assumed identity. Yet, according to the State's own assessment report, fingerimaging technology and its administration would cost 13 million dollars to implement and 5.2 million dollars to maintain annually. It was inconceivable to the supporters of these systems that the installation and maintenance costs of the fingerimaging technology would not outweigh, by far, any possible savings which this system might procure.

The New York State Department of Social Services claimed that the fingerimaging pilot project had saved taxpayers around $100,000 because the local DSS in Onondaga and Rockland Counties couldn't account for 145 Home Relief recipients out of 3,344 (4.3%) who had their cases closed when they failed to respond to a DSS request to be fingerprinted. Another 330 (9.9%) cases were closed for "routine reasons," including moving, excess resources, and client request. However, there are many reasons why people do not continue their case when it is time to recertify, including failing to receive the notice from DSS. The NYSDSS failed to provide any data comparing the normal rate of non-recertification to the 4.3% in the pilot counties. In Albany County, for instance, 800 Home Relief cases were being recertified each month. Of these, approximately 100 (12.5%) were closed for failing to recertify ("no contact"), and 50 (6.25%) were closed for other eligibility reasons, for a total of approximately 18.75% of all cases. In the two fingerprinting pilot projects the total number of recipients leaving welfare was only 14.2%. These figures suggested that fingerimaging had virtually no effect on detecting or deterring welfare fraud.

Proponents for fingerimaging welfare recipients pointed out that some individuals in our society were already being fingerprinted as a condition of their employment. However, this analogy was flawed due to the fact that these individuals could choose whether or not to be fingerprinted. From the perspective of those in the Forum, fingerimaging welfare recipients was a form of blackmail since it was not actually a matter of choice, but one of survival. If welfare applicants did not want to undergo fingerimaging, the alternative may well have been that they and their families would go hungry and homeless.

Almost half of the Home Relief population had serious medical and mental health problems. We imagined that an individual suffering from paranoia may not be willing to undergo fingerimaging. Groups representing victims of domestic violence said they feared that fingerimaging could have been used by their abusers to track them down. Also anyone with a previous criminal record might have been reluctant to have their fingerprints taken at a welfare office for fear of reprisals from the criminal justice system. Many people had already reached their toleration limits with a public assistance system that offered an insufficient monthly allowance, an inefficient application process, and that functioned to humiliate them and maintain them in poverty. For many in the Forum, fingerimaging represented the straw that would break the proverbial camel's back.

Those in the Forum who had experience with the welfare system reported that in the crowded and hectic environment of welfare centers there already was significant inappropriate disclosure of AIDS virus status and other information regarded as confidential. There was the real fear that a person's fingerimage along with the individual's confidential information stored in these systems might be shared with other government and corporate organizations. Although those proposing and implementing these fingerimaging systems claimed the print and the client information would be kept confidential, many remained skeptical.

Sr. Rita pointed out that one only had to refer to the similar claims made by social security when it began issuing the nine digit ID number to maintain deep suspicions regarding the limitations and confidentiality of government ID systems. When Social Security numbers were first used, their sole purpose was a narrow one—the opening of a social security account. Today, Social Security numbers are used on various kinds of licenses, college identification cards, bank accounts, loan applications and public assistance applications. They are also used by criminals to dip into bank accounts, take out credit cards under an assumed name, steal government benefits, or browse private college records and investment portfolios. In our estimation, information collected by government bureaucracies tended to proliferate—sometimes into the wrong hands. Fingerimaging information of welfare recipients was unlikely to be kept confidential for very long.

For the Forum, the fingerimaging of welfare recipients represented the intrusiveness of the governmental "Big Brother" into the lives of low-income people for the questionable social goal of scaring people away from government assistance. It was a form of social engineering which used intimidation and control to modify the behavior of the poor. The involuntary fingerimaging of public assistance recipients amounted to the criminalization of an entire class of people in our society—the poor. We asked: how would middle class citizens react if the U.S. government proposed to fingerprint Social Security recipients, or income tax filers? Yet, the rate of fraud and abuse in these systems far surpassed the cost of welfare fraud. It was our conviction that the philosophical basis used to justify the fingerimaging of welfare recipients was weak, whether one argued from the starting point of financial pragmatism, or from a more critical social theory. Sophisticated technological surveillance of the poor served the imaginary interests of political power and wealth. The members of the Forum were convinced we needed to resist these idols of security.

Initially, the form that this resistance took was a persistent disruptive presence at the monthly County Legislature meeting in the County Court House in downtown Rochester. For more than two years, the Forum, along with volunteers and guests from the House of Mercy, packed the public forums of the legislature's sessions with dozens of picket-laden protesters who would eventually line up at the open microphone and address their catatonic representatives. Month after month this queue of concerned citizens would recite the litany of offences which the proposed fingerimaging technology represented to those who received social service benefits. Month after month, a glazed-eyed Republican-dominated legislative body would scarcely tolerate our rude eruption of popular opinion. Like an episode from the Twilight Zone, there seemed to be some parallel, but separate, universe in which they were rendered insensate to the boisterous crowd arrayed before them. Ultimately, to no one's surprise, the legislature voted in favor of the fingerimaging technology which, in turn, sent the Forum back to the community organizing drawing board in order to revise our counter-fingerimaging strategy.

The strategy on which we finally settled was both simple and direct—picket and protest the implementation of the fingerimaging at the Monroe County Department of Social Services on the day of its installation. Other more extreme alternatives had been discussed, including a plan to highjack the van carrying the technology from New Jersey to Rochester, which had all the romance of a swashbuckling tale of piracy on the high seas. As entertaining as some of our other protest scenarios were, we settled on the more practical and, by far, better-rehearsed option of demonstration and picketing.

It was a cool and dreary late September morning and weary protesters had begun to accumulate in the DSS parking lot. Those of us who could be pleasant at that hour exchanged pleasantries. The rest of us struck mannequin poses with opium stares, propping our bodies at angles against the nearest fixed object waiting for the morning nourishment to kick in. Our numbers swelled significantly as the vans from the House of Mercy arrived and unloaded a more animated contingent who were laden with posters, signs and brochures that would be handed out to passersby. Sr. Grace called the Forum together for a last minute *ad hoc* organizational meeting. Grace looked determined and a little angry (her protest façade) as she addressed the assembled committee.

"Rita, Gloria and I spoke in the van on the way here and we've decided that something more needs to be done to demonstrate our outrage at this terrible offence to our friends and guests."

"Uh, oh," C.W. playfully interjected. Grace laughed, nudging C.W. and continued.

"After about ten minutes or so of protesting on the sidewalk out in front, Rita, Gloria and I have decided the three of us are going to go into the building and try to perform some symbolic act of protest in front of the newly installed fingerimaging hardware."

"But didn't we discuss this at the last meeting?" Greg said in a concerned tone. "And didn't we decide it was too risky 'cause the DSS warned everyone in that editorial they ran in the newspaper that trespassers would be arrested.?"

"That's right," Rita responded. "And we still believe that the rest of the protesters need to stay our here on the sidewalk. Grace, Gloria and I have decided we need to engage in some symbolic act of civil disobedience."

"We aren't exactly sure what that will be yet," Sr. Gloria chimed in. "We haven't seen the layout of the technology…heck, we don't even know which room it's in!"

"That's right," Sr. Grace added. "We may not get past the security at the door, but something more confrontational needs to be done. These Republicans and bureaucrats need to be directly challenged—face-to-face. We can't let them off the hook with a polite little obedient demonstration. We're going to take this protest off the streets and in through the front doors of the DSS!"

Being, for the most part, polite and obedient, the rest of us acquiesced to the last minute change in our plans. Then each of us picked out a sign, or grabbed a stack of flyers and staked out a spot on the sidewalk in front of the DSS building. Some reporters were there from the newspapers, but no television crews were there at the start of our protest. Grace conducted an interview with this group of reporters, as photographers snapped our pictures. Occasionally, a DSS worker or a person seeking benefits would walk by, but for the most part, protesters and those reporting on the protest dominated the event.

We watched nervously as Grace, Gloria and Rita walked toward the front doors of the DSS building. They made it though the front doors without so much as a pause and then disappeared down a hallway as they headed for the waiting room where DSS clients were processed.

After ten minutes, three police cars pulled in front of the DSS building—lights flashing and sirens blaring. Four officers stoically passed through the gauntlet of protesters and entered the building. Within a few minutes they reemerged with Grace, Gloria and Rita in custody, each with their hands cuffed behind their backs. The demonstrators fell silent as if holding a momentary vigil as the nuns passed by in review. Grace was the last to exit the building and as she approached us she began to shout anti-fingerimaging slogans, exhorting us to continue our demonstration. A few of us shouted back our support and love, but most of the protesters had been rendered silent by the spiritual and existential shock induced by witnessing our beloved nuns get escorted to prison in their separate police cars.

The demonstration was effectively over when the third police car pulled away with Grace in it. A fourth police car remained and the officers kept an eye on the rest of us as the protest gradually disintegrated—leaving piecemeal, vehicle by vehicle, in the same manner as we had arrived. Grace, Gloria, and Rita were released into the custody of their religious order later that day. The evening news ran a brief video clip of the nuns being taken into the police station. Richard Schauseil, the Director of the DSS, gave a condescending sound bite suggesting that the protesters were simply ignorant Luddites who did not understand the benefits of this complex technological advance that was poised to usher in a new era of fraud-free welfare. The next day newspapers ran the story on the second page of the "Local" section along with an extended commentary by the Director of the DSS defending the new fingerimaging systems. The reasoning behind our position in protest against fingerimaging, which Grace had carefully outlined for the reporter, was entirely missing.

At the December meeting of the Forum we approved Grace's idea of holding a community rally for the House of Mercy in the light of the political troubles it was facing regarding its practice of turning no one away. Originally, the rally was to be held in January, but delays crept into the plans, as they always do, and the rally was postponed until February 1997. It just so happened that the Mayor's investigation into the situation of the homeless in Rochester also became protracted. When he heard about the February rally at the House of Mercy, he called Grace a week beforehand and asked her if he could announce the findings of his research at that event. Grace agreed in spite of the fact that Mr. Johnson gave no indication regarding the conclusions of his research. Later in the week, a meeting between Sr. Grace, the Mayor and the superior of the Sisters of Mercy was set for the same afternoon as the rally. That meeting would determine the fate of the House of Mercy.

Sr. Grace and I spoke numerous times that week, but Grace remained largely in the dark concerning the Mayor's position and her anxiety was growing with each passing day. I tried to reassure her that the Mayor would never have agreed to speak at our rally if the news wasn't good, but Grace knew my condolences were only speculative. Rita, C.W. and Gloria mirrored Grace's heightened levels of stress and concern, each in his or her peculiar way. The Lenten Season was upon us in more ways than one and the somber mood at the House of Mercy was a fitting reminder of this season that emphasizes anxious waiting.

When I arrived at the House of Mercy I was just coming out of a planning meeting for Holy Trinity's staff which ran late. We were doing last minute planning for a Lenten program that had gotten a late start. I was hungry and a little dazed, still partly in the grip of the issues that surfaced at Holy Trinity. As I pushed the side door open I was struck by the bright lights for the television cameras and the sound of amplified speakers set up across the main lobby. The place was packed with House of Mercy guests, staff, community members, social workers from other agencies, nuns, reporters, and camera crews, all giving various levels of attention to the speakers and rally leaders. I wanted desperately to find out what had transpired so far, but no one I knew well enough to ask was near enough to me. I tried to get C.W.'s attention as he went about the task of orchestrating the rally, but my effort was to no avail. The crowd was too thick and there was enough enthusiastic, spasmodic, body movement on the part of most participants to dissuade any attempts to wade into the fray in search of a familiar face. I was afraid I had missed the Mayor's address, but a tall, tawny woman leaning against the desk next to me reassured me that the Mayor and the Sisters were still negotiating in the Conference Room.

Just then the crowd erupted in a great roar as Sr. Grace exited the Conference Room, which was situated in relation to the rally so that its door exited directly onto the rally's main stage. Grace smiled coyly in response to the cheers and then raised her arms over her head crying, "Good news!" The crowd roared again as C.W. ushered Grace to the microphone. She briefly composed herself and adjusted her hair. Then she addressed the assembly.

"Hi everyone. Thanks for coming," she said, eliciting an echo of the earlier roar from a crowd that wasn't yet prepared to listen in polite silence. Amused, Grace chuckled at the small outburst and continued.

"Your overwhelming response to our invitation tonight is more than encouraging. It is a sign that the House of Mercy plays an essential role in our community and that it touches the lives of many people in a way that is loving and life-giving."

Cheers rose again, both in response to Grace's words and because the Mayor, Bill Johnson, along with the others from the meeting were leaving the Conference Room. C.W. directed Grace's attention to the action that was going on behind her and she turned around to invite the Mayor to join her in addressing the rally. Grace gave the Mayor an extemporaneous introduction and then handed the microphone over to him.

"Good evening," the Mayor greeted the crowd which instinctively roared back its distinctive greeting. "It is my pleasure to announce to you this evening that the City, the Sisters of Mercy, and the House of Mercy have signed a memorandum of understanding regarding the continued operation of the House of Mercy as an emergency overnight shelter for the homeless." When the cheers from the electric crowd subsided the Mayor continued.

"Following weeks of intense discussion about the future of the facility, we have signed a document that outlines a course of action that will continue to address the needs of the homeless individuals at the House of Mercy, while properly addressing the safety and code issues that are of concern to the City. In December, City code inspectors found homeless individuals sleeping overnight at the House of Mercy, a violation of the zoned usage of the facility which was not equipped to handle overnight sleeping arrangements. As a result of that inspection and concerns by the City, the Sisters of Mercy set a deadline of January 24 to cease overnight shelter at the house. That deadline was given a two-week extension so that I could properly complete my personal investigation of the situation. Since that time it has become increasingly clear that the services provided by the House of Mercy address a significant gap in the community for the 'hard to serve' homeless population. While issues concerning safety and the appropriateness of accommodations cannot be ignored, both the City of Rochester and the Sisters of Mercy feel it is important to provide care for all homeless individuals, including those who may fall through the cracks. The 'Memorandum of Understanding' details what actions must be taken by the House of Mercy to bring the facility into compliance. As long as this course of action is followed, the City will allow the Sisters of Mercy to operate as a shelter until the facility is brought into full compliance."

As the Mayor spoke, C.W. pulled Grace aside and held his hand up to his ear, indicating she had a phone call. During the question and answer session with the Mayor that followed his address, C.W. discreetly retrieved Rita and Gloria from the crowd. After the question and answer period the Mayor dismissed himself and the rally continued with testimonials from guests and community members. During these testimonials, Grace, Rita and Gloria reappeared together on the main stage of the rally. C.W. took control of the microphone and reported that the sisters had something important to tell us. With a somber expression on her face, Sr. Grace took the microphone from C.W. and addressed the rally.

"I hate to dampen the spirit of such a wonderful outpouring of support," she said, with a smile that conveyed both affection and dismay. "However, Sr. Rita, Sr. Gloria and I have just been subpoenaed by the County of Monroe in the State of New York to stand trial for criminal trespass at the Monroe County Department of Social Services, when we protested the fingerimaging systems back in September." Boos and catcalls rose from the crowd as Sr. Grace called the rally back to order. "With your support, we're going to fight this thing and win, just like we've done all along. The idols of security and their worshippers will not win out over the God of love and justice."

Idols of security had plagued the House of Mercy for years. The delusions of security inspired by the fingerimaging merchants had consumed the better part of our organizing efforts for the past few years. Efforts to shut down the House of Mercy had treated zoning codes as ends unto themselves, and the homeless as a means to the political end of silencing that disturbing voice calling from the urban wilderness of Rochester's streets. The legal codes, which were designed to protect and ensure our security, became idols that were manipulated to serve as weapons in an ideological war against the poor. Ironically, it was a Roman Catholic organization that was battling these idols of security—an outreach that was born from the same Church that is often found struggling with its own penchant to dogmatically define and canonically legislate every ambiguity out of our religious lives. Nevertheless, the Judeo-Christian God always lies beyond the confines of our definitions, and God's love always reveals the inadequacies in our capacity to legislate security. The God of love, justice, mercy, forgiveness, hope and compassion serves as a spoil to our many and various idols that would claim we can secure what we need and desire by our own clever machinations.

The Trial

By the winter of 1998 the many and various worthwhile commitments that I had innocently undertaken over the past few years were collectively becoming an unwelcome imposition. Between the full time parish ministry, part time tennis instruction, advocacy on the board of a small credit union to lure it into my working class neighborhood and the treasury position on the neighborhood association board, there was precious little time to keep up with the goings on at the House of Mercy. I had been meaning to call Sr. Grace for weeks, but it always seemed to slip my mind during that window of opportunity when one was likely to catch Grace behind her desk—after two in the afternoon—and before 5:00pm when an *ad hoc* receptionist ended the day answering the main phone number. I knew in the back of my head that the court date for the trespassing case was coming soon, but I had lost track of the details. On this particular afternoon I had left myself numerous little reminders scattered all around my office in the rectory: on the phone, on the computer screen, in my daily calendar and even on the back of my desk chair. It was about three in the afternoon when I completed a bulletin announcement inviting potential confirmation candidates to sign up for sacramental preparation in the Parish office. I sat back in my desk chair and felt the cool stiffness and heard the crinkling sound of the full sheet of paper I had taped as a reminder when I left for lunch. Without hesitation I was on the phone dialing the House of Mercy. After a few rings an unfamiliar woman's voice answered the phone:

"House-a-Mercy." Before I could reply she pulled the handset away from her face and yelled at someone in the reception area who was making her laugh. "You hush up, yah hear? Can't you see I'm busy?" She shouted finishing with a deep-throated laugh. "Sorry baby, now what can I do for you?"

"Could I speak to Sr. Grace please?" I responded.

"Sr. Grace? Hang on," the receptionist said curtly as she placed me on hold. After two minutes of silence passed I was nearly convinced that I had been disconnected when the receptionist picked up my line again.

"House-a-Mercy."

"Yeah. I'm holding for Sr. Grace," I said in a slightly less patient tone.

"Sr. Grace? Hold please." She repeated her familiar formula, but before I could tell her that I had already been waiting for Sr. Grace she placed me on hold again. This time, however, my call was forwarded to Sr. Grace's office. C.W. answered the phone:

"House-a-Mercy, C.W. speaking."

"Hi C.W., it's Tom," I said.

"Hey stranger! What's up?" C.W. greeted me warmly.

"Well that's just it." I said. "I wish I wasn't some kind of stranger, but that's what I've become. I'm just calling to find out what's happening and get a handle on when Grace, Rita and Gloria are scheduled to appear in court."

"Well, no one can say you don't have a great sense of timing. The jury selection begins tomorrow," C.W. said with a hint of amusement in his voice.

After delivering some gratuitous apologies for my absence and consequent ignorance of this monumental event, I began pouring over my schedule. Suddenly, all of my "vital" commitments seemed negotiable and less significant. With a few strategic phone calls I could clear major blocks of time out of the next few weeks. In my own defense, the staff at the House of Mercy had been preoccupied for months preparing for the trespassing defense. Since I was not being called as a witness for the defense, I was not part of these preparations. My only personal contact with the House of Mercy in the previous six months had been the birthday party for Sr. Grace and Fr. Neil—an event treated like a high holy day by House of Mercy staff.

I was still trying to recover from my feelings of culpable alienation when C.W. made an announcement that exposed the extent of my absence.

"Oh, did you hear that Trick died? C.W. said cautiously. "You know we hadn't seen much of Tricky Dick in the past few months. Well, they found him dead in his apartment yesterday."

"God, that's awful," I said. "Did his drinking and drugging finally catch up with him?"

"Well, he certainly had gone back to the bad old habits these past couple of years," C.W. said. "The actual cause of death was liver failure. He also had AIDS and we couldn't give him his AZT and other AIDS medications towards the end because of the failing liver."

My thought process was momentarily stalled by the unexpected shock from the news of Tricky Dick's death. Although I knew the staff had been struggling with his behavior for some time, I had forgotten he had AIDS. Since he could not afford proper treatment, his return to alcohol and drugs helped relieve the physical suffering of the disease. I was trying to say something, but powerful memories of the man were disrupting the formation of intelligible language.

"Tom?" C.W. queried after an awkward period of silence.

"Yeah," I said in a hollow voice. "I was just thinking about Trick. It's a shame…what a shock."

"Well, if you had only seen him these past few months," C.W. said. "Most of us here were almost expecting something like this would happen sooner than later. He was always short of breath and gasping for air, and his stomach began to swell as a result of the liver damage. Two months before his death his roommate died of an overdose so there was no one to keep us informed about his health, or call the ambulance if there was an emergency. Near the end his father came up from Florida to see him. It was the first time in decades they had been together. He was just 54 years old. The funeral is tomorrow if you can make it."

I had a previous engagement and was unable to be present at Tricky Dick's sending off. I regretted not saying goodbye to this flawed guru of the streets. We had all hoped that Trick would be able to stay away from alcohol and drugs, but those chemical security blankets are difficult to resist. We also hoped he might live with AIDS indefinitely, like others who were on more sophisticated and costly treatments. But his treatments were mainly those he could purchase on a street corner, or scrounge from an equally desperate friend. Life was a trial for Tricky Dick, with a painful and punishing conclusion. He made the best of what he had been given, and that is the best that can be said of any of us. It was my prayer in the moment that this sage urban shaman would finally feel in the next life that love of his compatriots which may have slipped through his grasp in this one.

Upon entering the courtroom I was surprised to find it almost full. Due to a parking fiasco—during which I found and then subsequently rejected no less than four separate spaces before settling on one in the courthouse parking lot—I was late for the jury selection process so I found a seat near the back. I hunkered down into a dark inconspicuous corner from whence I could vicariously devour the courtroom action and its environs. Sr. Grace, Sr. Rita, Sr. Gloria and their lawyer Jim Gocker sat in fierce consultation at the front on my left. The prosecuting attorney was standing at the Judge's bench with the Judge, who was perched against the banister on the stairway leading up to his bench. They were locked in a give-and-take exchange that produced alternating expressions of thoughtfulness and puzzlement. The setting was grand in a kitchy sort of way. The entire room was decked in a mid-1970's wood paneling, giving it the feel of a very large finished basement. The bench itself looked like an oversized wet bar, and the overhead recessed lighting only reinforced this homely impression. My beaded nylon seat, the marble floor and the hung ceiling all gave loud testament to the decades old era when a contractor had last graced this courtroom. The only thing missing was the lime green carpet, which I was certain lay hidden behind one of the doors at the other end of the room leading into the Judge's chamber and the jury room.

As I sat there enumerating the countless violations of good taste on display at the center of Rochester's legal universe, a group of three young men entered through the doors on my far right each carrying what appeared to be electronic equipment. They walked to the front of the courtroom and met a fourth member of their party who had been seated in the front row. They consulted briefly and then began to set up tripods, cameras and other video production paraphernalia right next to the jury box. While I was used to the media's presence at all House of Mercy public events, this seemed like an unusual circumstance for any of the local television stations to be setting up shop. After all, weren't cameras banned from the courtroom? I wasn't really sure.

Just then, the prosecuting attorney returned to his bench and collected his papers, stuffing them in his briefcase. The Judge returned to the bench and turned on his microphone with a pop that reverberated throughout the room. Gratuitously, he called the relatively sedate room to order and then launched into an explanation of the procedure for jury selection. Each prospective juror would be individually summoned into the jury chamber through a door in back of the Judge's bench. There, both the defense and prosecuting attorneys would interview the juror. Jurors would then return to the courtroom and wait to find out whether they would be chosen to hear the case. Because Sr. Grace, the House of Mercy, and this specific case were so well known in the community, the court had anticipated a lengthy and difficult jury selection process. Finding twelve jurors who were not already biased would be plenty difficult enough. However, they also needed to find twelve unbiased jurors who would be willing to convict three Sister's of Mercy of felonious trespass.

After about twenty minutes I could see the better part of this day would be spent finding the right people to sit on the jury. So I began sneaking towards the front of the courtroom in order to wish the sisters well and be on my way to a lunch date at my neighborhood association. In the dimly lit courtroom the potential jurors sat shadowy and still like an audience awaiting the overture to some operatic tragedy. My gaze was fixed on the Sisters and Jim Gocker who were well lit by spotlights, like actors on a stage. I was composing my brief greeting and well wishes when a hand from the shadowy audience grabbed me by the left arm. Startled, I let out a grunt and jumped forward half a step. Turning to face my assailant I saw C.W. smiling sheepishly, apparently recognizing he had just given me a start. He invited me to sit down next to him, which I gratefully accepted.

"You lookin' for a place on the jury?" C.W. joked.

"I was about to ask you the same thing," I retorted. "Looks like jury selection is all they are going to get around to today."

"Today?!" C.W. said with genuine surprise. "This process might take us through the rest of this week!" The voice of experience said with conviction.

"Yikes! I'm glad I already made plans for today," I said.

"Yeah, you take pity on the rest of us back here cooped up in court when you're out there enjoying the balmy Rochester winter," C.W. said facetiously. He continued. "Jim Gocker's going to be very careful about who he lets on this jury. He's not just looking to filter out the ones who have biases and preconceived notions about the House of Mercy and Sr. Grace, he's also concerned about their attitudes toward freedom of speech and civil disobedience. He has a long series of questions—some of them are standard, but most are geared specifically to detect the kinds of prejudice that could work against us."

"Are all these people going to be interviewed?" I asked, looking around the room.

"All except the Court TV crew over there in the corner." C.W. answered.

"Is that who they are?!" I asked incredulously.

"Yup. I went over and talked to the guy in the front seat about an hour ago and he said they heard about this case only a week ago. This crew had to be assembled willy-nilly from other crews around the country. Some of them still haven't arrived; but he said they have enough equipment and personnel at least to begin doing some preliminary interviews. They're even going to interview me," he said, puffing his chest out in mock pride.

Resisting the temptation to take a cheap shot, I redirected our conversation to the defendants. "How are Grace, Gloria and Rita?"

"They're doing better than I thought they would," he said, and then added: "They're doing a hell of a lot better than I would. I've been really surprised by Gloria. I thought she'd be all nerves; but look at her; she's the picture of composure."

With that said I turned my attention back to the front of the courtroom. All three sisters looked calm, concerned and were engaged in a huddle among themselves, discussing trial strategy or something of that sort. I whispered a fond farewell to C.W. and continued my trek toward the front of the courtroom. As I approached the trinity, Grace was the first to see me out of the corner of her eye.

"Oh hey, look it's Tom!" Grace exclaimed as the nuns' conference disintegrated into a series of greetings and hugs. Grace was the first to stand and embrace me. Her hug was tighter and longer than usual. She was visibly moved by my modest demonstration of support. Rita was next to greet me. She was as warm, calm and good humored as she always was. Gloria greeted me with an unusual confidence and resolute determination. Although not the largest in stature or constitution, she appeared to be the one who was best prepared to face the prosecution.

I sat in the chair vacated by their lawyer, and Grace immediately began to fill me in regarding their experiences so far. She projected a nervous confidence as she covered all possible topics from what they had for breakfast at the House of Mercy that morning, to the detailed stage directions given to them by Jim Gocker in order to impress the Judge and jury while they gave testimony.

"Jim even told me not to fight with the prosecutor," said Grace with a half-sheepish, half-mischievous grin. "He said, 'just answer the questions and I'll redirect you if he's leading you in the wrong direction. Whatever you do, don't stand up and start yelling and pointing your fingers.' Who does he think he is?!" She concluded playfully.

"It certainly sounds like a boring trial to me," I said playing along. "Maybe you could yell and pound your fists, but remain seated and keep your digits to yourself."

"Did you know we're not supposed to stare at the jury," Sr. Gloria interjected. "Jim said that can be perceived as aggressive and intimidating."

"He even gave us suggestions about what to wear," Sr. Rita said in a tone that indicated her mild pique concerning matters of being told what to wear.

"It sounds like you're really well prepared and ready to take on any and all accusations from Richard Schauseil [the Director of the Department of Social Services]," I commented. The nuns agreed.

After answering a few questions about myself and other small talk and tidbits, I wrapped up my morning at court and made my way back out to my car, which was not parked on the street where I thought I had left it. After the initial panic and confusion subsided, I recalled where I had actually left the car and finally was on my way.

It would be three more days of jury interviews before I received a call from C.W. notifying me that the trial would begin the next day. For the next week I would be intermittently present for witness testimony. Their testimony was dominated by technical minutia, the purpose of which was to clarify that the nuns, either were (prosecution), or were not (defense), committing a felonious act of criminal trespass.

On the final day of testimony, Jim Gocker called the defendants to the stand. The first called was Sr. Gloria, who strode to the stand with unusual haste and resolve. The jury, whose leanings I had been trying to guess since the beginning of the proceedings, seemed to come to attention as Gloria took the stand. She answered most of Jim's questions 'yes' or 'no' in a loud, almost curt, manner. The normally soft-spoken and hesitating demeanor of Sr. Gloria was submerged beneath a more forceful and outspoken persona that morning. During cross-examination she maintained her composure, and when placed under duress, she even turned things up a notch. While never actually engaging the prosecutor in an argumentative battle, she more than held her own under questioning that was obviously intended to intimidate, confound and produce hesitation. If the sisters were going to look confused and unsure of themselves in front of the jury, it wasn't going to be accomplished during Gloria's testimony.

Sr. Rita was the next to be called to the stand. True to character, Rita took the stand calmly and deliberately, taking her seat in an erect posture, with her hands palms-down on the rail and chin held high.

In contrast to Gloria, Rita's answers to Jim's questions always seemed to be the outcome of careful consideration. There was always a brief, though perceptible pause between the conclusion of Jim's question and the beginning of Rita's response. This gave her testimony an honest and unrehearsed quality that undoubtedly reinforced the credibility of the defendant's version of the events. During cross-examination Rita added a matter-of-fact tone of incredulity to her voice when answering in the negative, which made the prosecutor's question seem silly or inconsequential. On more than one occasion Rita's response seemed to surprise the prosecutor enough to make him hesitate and fumble with his notes before composing himself for the next question. The sisters were now on the offensive.

The excitement rose as Jim Gocker called Sr. Grace to the stand. If nothing else, most of us recognized that this trial would soon be dealing with larger issues than the precise locations of the protesters in relation to DSS clients, or their relative cooperation with orders from Richard Schauseil and other DSS authorities. Through a series of leading questions, Jim guided Sr. Grace into a narrative of the morning of the protest from her perspective. Grace did not deny that she had knowingly entered the DSS premises against the will of the Director. She added that she believed that most of the clients were apparently there against his will since he was clearly driving them away using offensive surveillance techniques like fingerimaging. She did not deny that her protest might have temporarily impeded some clients from accessing their benefits. She added that about half of the clients present that morning had arrived with her in the caravan from the House of Mercy. She did not deny that she disobeyed the requests of Director Richard Schauseil to cease her protest and exit the public area of the Welfare Office. She added that it was her belief that an injustice was being committed against the poor and vulnerable, and she felt compelled to speak out on their behalf. It was her interpretation that Mr. Schauseil's order was an infringement of her constitutional right to free speech, and even if it wasn't, she felt compelled by her strong religious and moral convictions to speak out against what she perceived to be bullying tactics on the part of the Department of Social Services. She concluded:

"That morning I think we were doing what we, as Sisters of Mercy, were supposed to be doing—defending the poor. Catherine McAuley founded our religious congregation in order to serve the poor through justice, love and mercy. Sometimes having a mission of mercy means standing up and fighting against those who are brutal and merciless.

That's why we were there that morning—we were being Sisters of Mercy in the truest sense of the phrase."

In the moment of silence that ensued, I noticed a smile of appreciation form on the lips of a woman sitting in the front row of the jury box. Sr. Grace's statement seemed to have struck a chord. A different kind of smile—one of smug satisfaction appeared on the face of the prosecutor. The silence was broken by a cheering section of about forty guests from the House of Mercy who erupted in a flurry of "amens" and "you tell ums." The Judge restored order and leveled the threat of expulsion from the courtroom on anyone who dared to disrupt the proceedings again. Jim Gocker informed the court that his questioning had ended and he sat down. The Prosecutor's cross-examination was simple and perfunctory. He was obviously convinced that Sr. Grace's testimony had doomed the defense's case. He simply had Sr. Grace reaffirm that she had trespassed and obstructed the flow of services at the Welfare Office that morning, even after the Director had ordered her to move away from the service area and leave the building. For the prosecution, it now seemed like an open and shut case.

When Grace sat down, the Judge asked the defense if it had any more witnesses. The defense rested and both attorneys summed up their cases for the jury. The prosecution argued that according to numerous witnesses and the sister's own testimony, the defendants had indeed trespassed on government property and obstructed the flow of essential services. The defense countered on higher constitutional grounds that the sisters were exercising their freedom of speech and the defendant's commitment to their religious beliefs compelled them to acts of civil disobedience against the installation of a system of surveillance which stigmatized the poor. It was a daring defense since they could have taken the much simpler and safer route of arguing their innocence by finding and exploiting the technical differentia in the laws against criminal trespass. But the sisters saw the trial as more than simply a tedious exercise in legal intrigue. It was their pulpit, and they wanted to make a statement.

The jury began deliberation just before noon as the rest of us munched nervously on cafeteria food in the lobby just outside the courtroom doors. The television crew interviewed the sisters one by one, while well-wishers bid their fond farewells. Within two hours a remnant of about twenty hard-core supporters paced the marble floors rehearsing various fragments of the trial with their neighbor. After the entire trial had been rewound and played back far too many times, a somber hush fell over the assembled stakeholders. Most returned to pacing, or sat in dazed rumination. I dozed off in the middle of memorizing the complex pattern of ceiling tiles as I lay on one of the wooden benches.

I awoke with a start to find Fr. Neil sitting on the bench next to where my head rested, reading the newspaper.

"Welcome back sleepyhead. You've been out for almost an hour," he said, folding up his paper and adjusting his position on the bench. It was always difficult for Fr. Neil to sit comfortably due to a deformity in his hip, which also made it difficult for him to walk or stand for long periods. I checked my watch. It was almost 5:30pm. Six hours had passed since the jury began deliberating.

"Would it be stupid of me to ask if there has been any news?" I queried, as I sat up on the bench and readjusted my clothes and hair.

"No to both. But a small group of us is thinking about going out to pick up something to eat for the others. I think they're going to a fast food joint. What do you want? I'll tell C.W." Fr. Neil said this as he slowly and painfully stood up taking his wallet out of his pocket. By now I knew better than to argue with him regarding who would pay for a meal. Undoubtedly he would be paying for everyone's dinner tonight—including my own.

"Oh, I'm not picky. I'll just have what you're having," I said, knowing he would be nibbling on something insignificant and cheap.

"Well I'm just going to have a hamburger and a coffee. He said, predictably concerned that I wasn't eating enough. "Surely you'll want more than that. How about some fries? And you're not a coffee drinker. What about a Coke?"

"Ok, fries are fine, but I detest soft drinks. I'll just have water if all they have is coffee and soft drinks," I said, finishing my order.

With that Fr. Neil hobbled away flashing cash in the direction of C.W. who was busy taking orders from half a dozen other people at the doorway across the expansive lobby. Sr. Grace had finished giving her order and she appeared to be looking for a place to rest and get away from the crowd. Seeing me sitting alone in an inconspicuous place, she made her way over and sat down next to me. We hadn't spoken since the end of the trial so we were anxious to get each other's perspective on it.

"So what do you think?" She asked, obviously referring to the trial.

"Regardless of the outcome, you, Rita and Gloria made your point loud and clear," I said.

"Good...Jim says we're going to appeal a guilty verdict," said

Grace, updating my ignorance of the inner-circle strategies.

"You know," I began thoughtfully, "you did choose a risky defense strategy, but I think it was the right one. Not only from a position of principle, but also from the perspective of strategy. I think your testimony moved a few jurors. There was a woman on the jury who smiled and nodded during your final statement. I'll bet the jury is debating more than just the particulars of the law of criminal trespass."

"I hope so," said Grace in an unusually pensive manner. After a momentary pause she continued. "Did you know Carrie Goings died this past August?"

"Oh my God! No. She was so young…wasn't she?" I asked in shock, knowing she was rather young and healthy the last time I saw her.

"She was in her mid-thirties," Grace explained. "She died of breast cancer. She spent her last days at a nearby hospice. Just before she died I found her on the street wandering aimlessly—depressed. I brought her home to die…Do you remember her son?"

"Do you mean Darnell, the one who was always running away from foster homes and trying to reunite with his mom and siblings?" I responded.

"Yes," Grace continued. "He was so distressed about his mother's death that he shot himself in the face. We held his funeral just a few weeks ago at the House of Mercy. He came to visit her while she was sick. It was good to see them reunited, if only for a brief and sad moment. We think he believed that his death would somehow bring them together again in the afterlife."

"How tragic. What a sad tale," I concluded.

We sat silently together replaying images of the dead in our minds—sending spontaneous petitions on their behalf to a spiritual realm that we hoped would be a resting place and not just one more trial. Carrie's short life in this world had been a cruel and unusual sentence, prosecuted in a most brutal and unforgiving way. When the trials of this life are meted out so abundantly and inequitably on some of us, like Carrie Goings, one wonders whether there is compensation in a life beyond this one. It must have been experiences like this an others like it that inspired our traditional Catholic concepts of the afterlife. A sense of fairness must have motivated belief in a place where souls met different fates, somehow accomplishing justice in a cosmic realm, when on earth it had so obviously failed. If God is merciful, and justice does compensate for inequities in this life with countervailing rewards in the next, then Sr. Grace and I were wasting our time worrying about

Carrie Goings and her son Darnell.

Cold fast food dinners arrived in a not-so-fresh state because the van's carburetor had flooded in the McDonald's parking lot and they had to wait a half hour before they could restart the engine. Like cats who snub canned cat food that has been open too long, our hunger-inspired enthusiasm was terminally altered by the cooling down and gassing off of the special sauces and aromas. The magic produced by the flavor and odor manufacturers wears off rather quickly, revealing the sickening truth about the nature of one's fast food repast. Most of us spent the dinner hour in disappointed silence, forcing down tasteless lumps as if we were enduring a particularly harsh penance.

For the next three hours the nervous mood in the lobby shifted from excitement to pensiveness as the one real issue in the room became the length of time of the deliberations. They had been in there seven hours…eight hours…nine hours, and still no word. Finally, at ten minutes after nine, an officer of the court appeared at the courtroom door summoning us to return. We surmised that the Judge was calling us in to declare a recess until the next morning, but no sooner had we arrived then the Judge announced that the jury had reached a decision. The officer of the court summoned the jury, which promptly filed back into the jury box. The tension was so high in the court that we held our collective breath. Thankfully the Judge wasted no time asking the jury what verdict they had reached. The courtroom erupted in celebration when the "not guilty" verdict was read to the court. Even the poker-faced Judge seemed palliated—cracking a smile and releasing a sigh of relief—probably celebrating the fact that he had not been placed in the awkward position of sentencing three nuns for criminal trespass.

Amidst the solace and elation that ensued, it was difficult to see the larger significance of this decision, yet this trial had accomplished something extraordinary. In effect, the judicial system was establishing much more than the mere innocence of three nuns in regards to charges of criminal trespass. Because the nuns had chosen to defend themselves by appealing to higher principles of justice and freedom of speech, the court had, in effect, agreed that they were doing precisely what they were supposed to be doing that morning at the Department of Social Services. Although no one, not even the defense, argued that civil laws had been breached during the protest, the jury agreed with the nuns that when justice and mercy were being compromised it was sometimes appropriate for certain citizens to conscientiously disobey those laws in pursuit of those higher purposes. It was a day when heaven rejoiced in unison with those of us here on earth. Once again I had a vision of

God dancing joyfully, with her big black arms waving wildly over her head. She said,

> "Behold you who have endured the trial.
> Behold Tricky Dick and Carrie Goings.
> Behold Sr. Grace, Sr. Rita and Sr. Gloria.
> Behold the lamb who appeared to be slain."

Farbridge

It was early June 2001 and I was planning a trip which would take me back through Rochester. I was eager to be reunited with my friends from the House of Mercy, but I also had another motive for visiting. A few months ago, seemingly out of the blue, I began writing about my experiences with the House of Mercy. At first, the purpose of these memoirs was to stimulate ideas for more scholarly theological reflections. However, the project was taking on a life of its own. For years students had been urging me to record the stories I told them in class. Stories always seem to capture the moral imagination better than abstract theories and principles, so I often use narrative to illustrate an ethical point.

Every Spring semester at St. Gregory's University in Shawnee, Oklahoma, a course in moral theology is taught. Given my academic background, responsibility for teaching this course fell to me. I had moved to Oklahoma in the Summer of 1999 when a teaching position opened at St. Gregory's in the theology division. I was thrilled that I had found a full time position teaching in a college, even though it meant uprooting and relocating to a distant and foreign place. My adopted families at the House of Mercy and Holy Trinity Parish gave me a warm and enthusiastic *bon voyage* and two days later on an oven-hot, desert-dry day I arrived in Shawnee, Oklahoma in late July.

Over the next couple of years I had become the chair of the theology division, the director of the spirituality center, and taught a five-course, full time load. St. Gregory's was small and it seemed everyone was wearing more than one hat. My time at St. Gregory's had been rewarding and exciting, but it was quickly coming to an end. DePaul University in Chicago had advertised for someone to teach Catholic Social Thought starting in the Fall of 2001. The notice sounded so enticing that I felt compelled to throw my hat into the ring. Six months later, I was now struggling to find a reasonably affordable place to live. This trip home was actually just a roundabout stop on the way to the big city where I would take my search off the internet and onto the streets.

I arrived at 725 Hudson Avenue around 2:00pm on an ordinary Thursday afternoon. The reassuring familiarity of my surroundings was inviting as I found my customary parking space in back of the van on the side street next to the building. As I got out of my car I saw a man frantically escorting a little girl down Hudson Avenue towards Prince, who was leaning against the van talking to one of the volunteers. The girl was holding her arm and was letting out breathy grunts with each step. She had a preoccupied expression on her face and seemed to be concentrating intensely on some conundrum. I gathered from the conversation that the girl had fallen hard on the sidewalk and the man thought she might have broken her arm. He didn't know the girl, but he witnessed the fall and he knew Sr. Rita at the House of Mercy was a registered nurse, so he did the neighborly thing and brought her here. Prince whisked the girl past me toward the back door of the House of Mercy. On the way past he caught a glimpse of me and interrupted his interview of the little girl to say, "Hey Tom, long time no see." I responded, "Hey Prince…talk to you later when your hands are less full." Some things never change, and 725 Hudson Avenue is one such place where mercy endures forever.

Prince nodded acknowledging my response while maintaining his focus on the needs of the girl. I followed Prince at a more leisurely pace down the back driveway and into the back entrance which led up a short stairway into the kitchen. The funky atmosphere bluntly struck senses that had grown unaccustomed to the witch's brew that accumulates over the years in circumstances where the huddled masses congregate and cleaning simply can never be first on the priority list. I wound my way through labyrinthine hallways, smiling and nodding at the gauntlet of animatronic strangers who littered the way. I noticed that new vinyl tiles replaced the old sheet vinyl that originally had been lain in the halls. The old holes in the walls had been patched and replaced by new ones. The hung ceiling drooped intermittently and missing tiles revealed pieces of the jumbled network of water, gas, and electrical conduit. As the hallway coursed towards Grace's office, it sloped inexplicably downward, so that one had to check one's momentum like a mountaineer descending a steep trail.

Sr. Grace's hollow door rattled so much as I knocked that it sounded more like someone attempting to break in than someone just looking for a little attention. A heavyset man in his thirties who wore a tank top and a hairnet answered the door. Accustomed to playing the role of gatekeeper, he looked at me suspiciously. I explained that I was an old friend of Sr. Grace from out of town. Grace apparently overheard my explanation.

"Tom! Is that you? Come on in."

The century stepped aside and held the door open long enough for me to pass and then promptly shut it so no more riff-raff could interrupt the goings on at the House of Mercy nerve center. Grace and I exchanged hugs, greetings and pleasantries. Then she introduced me to Alan Morrell, a reporter from the Democrat and Chronicle who was interviewing Grace about a recent neighborhood incident in which a toddler died. I sat in the open seat against the wall at the left corner of Sr. Grace's desk, while Alan sat at the other corner taking notes as Grace gave her perspectives concerning this tragedy. I had not heard about this incident so I listened carefully and began piecing the story together from the fragmented question-and-answer format.

A six-year-old boy and his three-year-old brother were at a baseball game at their aunt's house. According to the children who witnessed the beating, the three year old threw a stone striking his brother, angering him. In turn, the older sibling hit the three year old in the lower body with a brick and then repeatedly struck him in the abdomen with a wooden baseball bat using overhead strikes. None of the other children intervened. Grace recalled that the children often played quite rough.

The children were eventually taken back home around 5:30pm where they were met by their mother's boyfriend who often babysat for them. The boyfriend was puzzled by the toddler's quiet behavior and his lack of appetite. He appeared very lethargic and he soon fell asleep on the couch while watching television. The babysitter then bathed both children and put them to sleep. While bathing the three year old the boyfriend did not notice any bruises or other injuries that might have alerted him to the toddler's critical condition.

That night the children slept together in the same bed as they usually did. The next morning when the family awoke, they found the three year old dead in his bed. Police believed he died early in the morning since rigor mortis had set in by the time they arrived.

Sr. Grace described the three year old as a cute, loving little boy who charmed everyone. According to Grace, he was always happy.

"It's very hard for the mother. She's holding it in. We're trying to get her to cry," Sr. Grace said, trying to put a human face on this gruesome incident. "Somehow in all this tragedy, something good will come out of it. God will bring good from this tragedy. We will hold them in our prayers, and we will support them," she concluded.

The reporter thanked Sr. Grace as he packed away his mini-cassette recorder and clipboard. Grace asked the century with the hairnet to escort the reporter through the maze of hallways back to the outside world.

After a second exchange of greetings and "great-to-see-yahs" Sr. Grace began to give me updates concerning the kinds of things that had happened at the House of Mercy over the last two years.

"You know about Farbridge House right?" She said, seemingly ready to dismiss the topic as common knowledge.

"No. I've never heard of it," I said apologetically.

"You haven't?!" Grace said, perplexed by my ignorance. "Oh, that's right, you probably left for Oklahoma before we opened Farbridge House…When did you go to Oklahoma?"

"July of 1999," I answered.

"Well that was right around the time Farbridge House was donated to us." Grace surmised. She continued. "Oh Tom, you should see the wonderful work that goes on over there. C.W. and my brother run the place. It's a halfway house for drug addicts from the House of Mercy who are ready to turn their lives around and get off alcohol and drugs once and for all. They won't take just anybody. The person has to demonstrate commitment to the process of becoming clean and sober. Do you remember Slim?" She asked.

"Yeah, the fifty year old man with the eighteen year old body," I replied.

"Well he's almost sixty now," said Grace parenthetically. "He's been sober for almost two years!" She said with genuine excitement.

"That's…amazing," I said, somewhat shocked to discover that this man who had once been perpetually high would have even been considered a serious candidate for such a program.

"There are so many success stories in this program and it's only in its second year," Grace continued. "There are six men living there now and a couple are getting ready to transition out and begin living on their own. Some of these men were our hardest core abusers of alcohol and drugs. What Neil and C.W. have done is nothing short of a miracle. God has surely blessed this program."

As Sr. Grace finished her description of Farbridge House Sr. Gloria came into Sr. Grace's office. Warm greetings and salutations were exchanged followed by a brief business meeting between Grace and Gloria. Gloria had just returned from the Sister's of Mercy Mother House. She and C.W. had gone together in the van. Gloria had gone to meet with Sr. Sheila while C.W. took the van to be repaired by the motherhouse mechanic. I entertained myself on the "new" computer in Grace's office while Sr. Gloria and Sr. Grace conducted their business. After a couple of hands of hearts, C.W. entered the office and a third round of warm greetings and salutations were exchanged. Grace had questions for C.W., but first he had a few for me.

"Do you know anything about AOL and email?" C.W. queried.

"Well, only the basics. I had an account with them a long time ago. Things have probably changed drastically," I replied.

C.W. sat down next to me and took hold of the mouse, clicking around a little bit and trying to find words to express a computer problem that was, on one level, simple, but on a more practical level, sounded hopelessly idiosyncratic. C.W. left me to my own devises while he and Sr. Grace briefed one another regarding a litany of practical issues. I made a number of half-hearted attempts to connect to the internet and then returned to what I knew best on the computer—solitaire. In the middle of a hand that appeared to be a sure winner, I noticed a commotion swirling around me. Eventually I heard my name.

"Tom…Tom!" Sr. Grace yelled.

"Yeah, oh sorry. I got caught up in the game," I finally responded.

"You remember Slim don't you?" She said by way of reintroduction as she gestured toward a tall gray-haired African American man in dapper attire standing at the doorway waiting to shake my hand. He stood tall and proud, looking me straight in the eye, sharing a big smile and a hearty hello. This was not the Slim stored in my memory banks: a listless, apathetic, disheveled, clownish, shy person who was in great shape, but who was perpetually immersed in one kind of haze or another. We shook hands and sat down while he told me all about Farbridge House and how his life had changed as a result of this new outreach. Slim made frequent glowing references to C.W. who responded in his characteristically modest manner, which belied the profound impact he has had on his peers and co-workers. He also outlined the structure of their week at Farbridge that included regular one-on-one and group counseling sessions with Fr. Neil. At the end of his presentation I asked if I could see Farbridge House. Everyone momentarily looked at each other seeking a definitive answer to my query. Then C.W. stood up and said:

"Well let's go. I haven't got all day. We'll stop by Farbridge on our way to OLPH. It's just around the corner."

Sr. Grace and Gloria remained behind as C.W. chauffeured Slim and me to our separate destinations. It turned out that Farbridge House was named after Farbridge Street where it was located. The cube van in which we rode was virtually new and was clearly a departure from the norm at the House of Mercy. When I commented on some of its many luxurious features C.W. promptly pointed out that this van had been purchased with the help of money I had procured years ago through grants I had written. I thought C.W. was kidding since it had been my impression that my grant writing efforts had been entirely fruitless. C.W. assured me he was not kidding and then went on to list a number of other grants that I had written which had ultimately been funded. I was momentarily flush with pride and a deep feeling of satisfaction enveloped me. As I basked in the glow of my newly discovered success, the van came to a stop in front of a modest two-story colonial home on a short unassuming side street.

Slim, who was sitting in the front passenger seat, grabbed C.W.'s right hand with his left and gave it a firm squeeze thanking him for the ride and wishing him farewell. He then shot me a glance and threw a short wave in my direction saying it had been good to see me once again. As I returned Slim's sentiments, C.W. asked if I would like to tour the premises.

"There's really not much to see—just an ordinary house," C.W. said. "Slim is the only one there right now so you wouldn't get to meet any of the community members."

I declined this half-hearted invitation, sensing in C.W. an urgency to get me to OLPH so that he could get back to what he needed to do at the House of Mercy. On the short drive to OLPH, C.W. reiterated the basic philosophy of Farbridge which Grace had explained earlier, injecting greater detail concerning the rather disciplined routine expected from the residents. No one was allowed to loiter in the neighborhood or sit around the house all day. These were behavior patterns which often preceded a return to addiction. All of the residents were required to attend Alcoholic Anonymous or Narcotics Anonymous meetings at least once per week, and everyone was encouraged to develop a spiritual life of their own choosing.

As the van lurched up the ramp into the OLPH parking lot, C.W. informed me that he would be seeing me at dinner that evening. I stood in the parking lot watching the van turn around, happily admiring that which I had procured through my grant-writing efforts. I rang the rectory door bell once again, concerned that maybe the secretary had gone home for the day and Fr. Neil had possibly left on an emergency, leaving me to fend for myself until his return. I knew my worries were in vain when I saw through the sheer curtain on the door a slow moving figure negotiating the small flight of steps leading down to the entryway. Fr. Neil's health had been poor throughout the last year and only a few weeks before he had been hospitalized. Sr. Grace said even the doctors feared he wouldn't recover; but now here he was, only three weeks later, back in the saddle preparing to celebrate liturgy and then take the gang out for dinner.

After warm welcomes Fr. Neil excused himself so that he could prepare for the five o'clock liturgy. He invited me to join the celebration, but warned it would be conducted in Spanish. While I was not put off by the Hispanic celebration, I declined because I was exhausted and nearly asleep on my feet. Instead I found a big, soft chair in the rectory reception room and promptly fell fast asleep in the plump, cozy silence.

On our way to dinner that evening, Fr. Neil and I caught up with each other. His illness had been more serious than I had believed, but he and his doctor were confident that his recovery was complete. He had agreed to serve only one more year in parish ministry for the Diocese of Rochester and then he could dedicate himself completely to the Farbridge mission. The ministry had a waiting list of over a dozen men and was already on the verge of purchasing a second property. Future plans included the acquisition of a farm in the Southern Tier of the State where the more hard-core cases could get away from city distractions and temptations, as well as deconstruct the network of suppliers on which most dedicated addicts depend. The ministry even had identified a prospective farm as well as a generous donor willing to fund such a purchase. Fr. Neil's face was alive with excitement and his eyes sparkled as he relayed the vibrant details of this growing ministry.

His narrative continued as we pulled into the parking lot and walked into the restaurant through the fresh temperate air of this late spring evening. The sun blazed low on the horizon and a warm breeze caressed our faces as if someone had imported a Tahitian sunset, so that, for just one night, weather weary Rochesterians could bask in such exterior comforts. It was a shame that the rest of our party was inside. If only we had chosen a restaurant with outdoor seating, we mused, as we drank deeply one more time from this climactic treat before abandoning it for the stale drab of interior spaces. Inside the party raged and soon Fr. Neil and I were swept up in the festive spirit of the evening.

That night I lay awake in my bed staring out at the starry sky, reflecting on how I could best express my experience of this unique gift to the church. It occurred to me that in every age God offers us brief snapshots of the possibilities in our faith which normally lay dormant. Our experience of the gospel is usually so filtered through non-gospel layers of our existence that its essence gets lost, or at least easily dismissed. Usually we mistake it for something other than itself— normally something more comfortable and much easier to achieve. I felt blessed to have been a witness to one of these less mitigated manifestations of God's reign.

Like so many before them, the staff at the House of Mercy put flesh on the text of the gospel. They share the hospitality of which Henri Nouwen speaks so eloquently—creating a welcoming space for those who are the ultimate stranger among us. They also transparently demonstrate the tender courage which Catherine McAuley believed should be the cornerstone virtue of her Sisters of Mercy. The same spirit seems to be at work in the seventeenth century Jesuit-Guarani societies that thrived for almost one hundred years in South America. Here the Jesuits who accompanied the conquerors to the new world stubbornly insisted on recognizing the humanity—the *Imago Dei*— of those who had been dehumanized. Again the naked gospel was observed among the mendicants of the thirteenth century Western Europe whose embrace of poverty became an identification with the poor. The examples naturally took me back to the earliest Christian communities and the stories they told about a spirit-filled human being, who did not sit on a throne commanding massive armies and untold wealth, but ate and drank as a commoner, choosing to share the lot of the poor and outcast.

Somehow it is somewhere in communion with the poor that Christianity rediscovers and reinvents itself time and again, throughout the ages, and across the globe. Most of the time these movements have been tiny, localized manifestations which were subsequently lost to the historical record. Most of the time their witness has fallen on deaf ears and they have been treated like outcasts or curiosities. Sometimes they paid for their audacity with their lives. No matter their fate, one thing is certain, all of these movements challenged the established social and ecclesial structures with practices that upended the normative hierarchical distinctions and aggressively affirmed our essential dignity and equality before a higher power.

The House of Mercy gives God reason to dance, because in their little corner of this enormous world, God is allowed to be God. Here, God is not merely a name invoked to appease the superstitious crowds, or an ideological weapon wielded for the sake of social and ecclesial control. Here, God is not a ventriloquist doll, out of which spews our favorite concepts and beliefs. That's because at the House of Mercy people are not in the habit of manipulating "God." Here God reigns, not as a medieval European monarch, but as a contemporary African American matriarch. And here, in the funkiest of places, to the sounds of the funkiest music, God continues to dance victoriously.

About the Author

Dr. Thomas OBrien is an assistant professor of Catholic social thought at DePaul University and author of the book John Courtney Murray in a Cold War Context.

The direction of his work is especially influenced by the issues of homelessness, poverty and destitution. Therefore, themes of communal and social justice infuse the creative projects he pursues. The thrust of his commitment to social justice is inspired by what is known as the preferential option for the poor: a belief that God, through human agents, restores equality in the human family by literally undermining the structures of inequality and oppressionfavoring those who matter least in these hierarchies.

He recently published an article about the Jesuit/Guarani Missions in 17-18th century Paraguay titled Utopia in 17th Century Paraguay: A Reexamination of the Jesuit/Guarani Missions. This article is part of a theological project that examines Christian history in order to uncover instances of Christian communities embracing the central tenets of Catholic social thought.

Printed in the United States
24283LVS00005B/1-84